DATE DUE

DEMCO, INC. 38-2931

NOVALIS

NOVALIS

Philosophical
Writings

Translated and Edited by
Margaret Mahony Stoljar

STATE UNIVERSITY OF NEW YORK PRESS

Published by
State University of New York Press, Albany

For information, address State University of New York Press,
State University Plaza, Albany, N.Y. 12246

Production by Cathleen Collins
Marketing by Fran Keneston

Library of Congress Cataloging in Publication Data

Novalis, 1772–1801.
    [Selections. English. 1997]
    Philosophical writings / Novalis ; translated and edited by
Margaret Mahony Stoljar.
        p.   cm.
    Includes bibliographical references and index.
    ISBN 0–7914–3271–8 (alk. paper). — ISBN 0–7914–3272–6 (pb : alk.
paper)
    1. Philosophy.   I. Stoljar, Margaret Mahony.   II. Title
B3071.A35N68   1996
193—dc20   96–16782
                                                        CIP

10 9 8 7 6 5 4 3 2 1

Philosophy cannot bake bread—but it can bring us God, freedom, and immortality.

I show that I have understood a writer only when I can act in his spirit, when, without constricting his individuality, I can translate him and change him in diverse ways.

Novalis

Contents

Acknowledgments

The texts translated were selected from the German critical edition of *Novalis Schriften*, edited by Richard Samuel with Hans-Joachim Mähl and Gerhard Schulz, vols. 2–3. Stuttgart: W. Kohlhammer, 1965–1968. The commentaries in this edition are invaluable. Other editions providing additional analysis of the texts are *Novalis Werke*, edited by Gerhard Schulz, Munich: C. H. Beck, 1969; and *Novalis, Werke, Tagebücher und Briefe Friedrich von Hardenbergs*, vol. 3, edited by Hans-Joachim Mähl and Richard Samuel, with Commentary by Hans Jürgen Balmes, Munich/Vienna: Carl Hanser, 1987. I have relied extensively on all these editions.

I wish to thank Emeritus Professor Gerhard Schulz of the University of Melbourne, for his kind encouragement and his help in clarifying many passages. I am grateful for the constructive suggestions made by Professor John Neubauer of the University of Amsterdam and Professor Steven Paul Scher of Dartmouth College.

Grateful acknowledgment is made to Kohlhammer Verlag, Stuttgart, for permission to translate a selection from the copyrighted works first published in *Novalis Schriften*.

Abbreviations

Introduction

The writer we know as "Novalis" was born in 1772 as Friedrich von Hardenberg. The manuscripts translated in this volume were compiled between late 1797 and late 1799, most remaining unpublished. The striking range of interests displayed in his notes, philosophical fragments, and short essays reveals Novalis to be one of the most comprehensive thinkers of his generation. He shared in the belief of his contemporaries in the psychological and social value of philosophy, poetry, and the other arts, but since he had also been educated in mathematics and the physical sciences, the dimensions of his writing are far-reaching.

His intellectual profile resembles that of an eighteenth-century polymath such as Diderot or d'Alembert, who wrote expertly on a myriad of scientific and cultural subjects. Indeed, Novalis's own unfinished project for an encyclopedic work, his *General Draft*, demonstrates his affinity with the *philosophes* whom he admired, even while rejecting their materialism. In spite of the boldness, rigor, and extensive scope of Novalis's intellectual pursuits, his philosophical work has been largely obscured for those who have thought of him as a prototypical Romantic dreamer. The popularity of his *Hymns to the Night*, a set of dithyrambic poems in verse and prose, and of his novel *Heinrich von Ofterdingen*, the source of the Romantic archetype of the blue flower, symbol of love and longing, does not prepare the reader for material such as is found in his philosophical manuscripts.

In his original, unprejudiced, and undogmatic questioning of any issue that interests him, Novalis displays to a remarkable degree the kind of innovative thought that will characterize the Romantic movement

1

throughout Europe. Being a practicing scientist and creative writer as well as possessing a comprehensive approach to theoretical inquiry that in his time was what was meant by "philosophical," Novalis engages with a wider spectrum of questions than do most of his contemporaries. But it is his readiness to subject any philosophical concept to radical interrogation that marks his published and unpublished work as of enduring interest. For contemporary readers accustomed to the critique of the categories of reason that has followed in the wake of Nietzsche, Novalis's writings can seem uncannily pertinent. They address issues that in recent years have continued to expand the parameters of our thinking on truth and objectivity, language and mind, symbol and representation, reason and the imagination. In form and style too, Novalis's manuscripts demonstrate the associative fluidity of thought characteristic of Nietzsche. They proceed by intuitive and imaginative reasoning, rather than sustained systematic argument, in a manner that has become familiar in the writing of Derrida and others in our time. His adoption of the Romantic fragment, a self-conscious and self-contained short prose form created in particular by Friedrich Schlegel to allow maximum flexibility in working out new and developing ideas, is ideally suited to his own quicksilver movement between subjects. In looking at the most important of his themes, it will be appropriate as well to point to the affinities between his approaches and his philosophical style and some of those current today.

Friedrich von Hardenberg was born in central Germany at Oberwiederstedt, in the region of Halle. As the eldest son of a family belonging to the minor aristocracy, Friedrich was tutored at home. He grew up in a household presided over by a devoted mother and a deeply religious father with close ties to the Moravian Brethren of Herrnhut in Saxony. A strong sense of family as the primary community and model for all others, as well as the pietist emphasis on personal faith and mystical communication with God, were aspects of Hardenberg's early years that proved to be enduring elements of his thought. While a law student at Jena, Leipzig, and Wittenberg between 1790 and 1794, Hardenberg made the acquaintance of Schiller, Friedrich Schlegel, and Fichte, and began to write poetry. Schiller, a historian and philosopher as well as a poet and dramatist, was, with Goethe, one of the two preeminent literary figures of the age. Schlegel, himself still a student, was to be a leader in the field of aesthetics and cultural theory in the late 1790s, at the center of a group that came to be known as the Romantic school.

The next three years saw Hardenberg engaged in intensive philosophical study, principally devoted to Kant and especially Fichte, whose writings, above all his *Theory of Scientific Knowledge* (1794), were received with enthusiasm by the young generation. His interest in mathematics and science, especially geology and mining, was stimulated by his father's appointment as director of the Saxon saltworks, and Hardenberg decided to embark on a course of study at the celebrated mining academy in Freiberg. Meanwhile he had been profoundly moved by the deaths of his young fiancée Sophie von Kühn and his brother Erasmus. These experiences, and the shadow of tuberculosis that lay over countless young people of his own age, prompted Hardenberg to a kind of mystical meditation on death and the possibility of resurrection, themes that became the subject of the poetic cycle *Hymns to the Night*. Late in 1797 he devoted himself intensively to study of the Dutch philosopher Hemsterhuis, whose concept of a moral sense and emphasis on the cognitive validity of poetic language and of feeling impressed him profoundly. He recorded his studies of Kant, Fichte, and Hemsterhuis in a number of philosophical notebooks, the first in a series that was to be continued throughout his life.

In the short years that remained before his death in March 1801, Hardenberg steeped himself in all aspects of contemporary thought, often exchanging ideas with the Schlegel circle, among whom was the philosopher Schelling. He continued to write poetry and prose fiction, as well as to explore philosophical, aesthetic, mathematical, and scientific topics in his notebooks. After completing his studies in Freiberg, Hardenberg became engaged to be married for a second time and applied successfully for a position as district administrator in Thuringia. However, late in 1800 his health began to fail rapidly and it became apparent that tuberculosis would defeat his hope of marriage and plans for further philosophical and literary works.

In the winter of 1797–1798, during his first months in Freiberg, Hardenberg prepared a collection of fragments, *Miscellaneous Observations*, as his first philosophical publication. It initially appeared under the title *Pollen*, and was signed with the pseudonym "Novalis," which means "one who opens up new land." The name had traditional associations with the Hardenberg family, but was particularly apt in view of the author's description of his own work as "literary seedings." This was Novalis's interpretation of the concept of *Symphilosophie*, or collaboration in philosophy, by which the Schlegel circle characterized their joint work as a kind of philosophical conversation. The Romantic fragment, sometimes brief and aphoristic, sometimes extended to several paragraphs, was conceived by its practitioners as specially suited to collaborative work, but the form also allowed Novalis to move in free association across any aspect of intellectual life. The idea of cultivating and fertilizing new land was evoked in the imagery of the published title, *Pollen*, and the epigraph to it: "Friends, the soil is poor, we must sow abundant seeds/ So that even modest harvests will flourish." These metaphors make explicit Novalis's concept of philosophical discourse not as something closed and finite but as a dynamic movement of thought. During the first half of 1798 Novalis continued to work on his philosophical notebooks; two selections from these unpublished manuscripts are translated here under the heading *Logological Fragments*.

Belief in spirituality, the conviction of human otherness as against the animal and inanimate worlds, is the grounding axiom of Novalis's thought. The hierarchy of spiritual value is extended by the positing of a higher realm of pure spirit, removed in kind from the human as much as the latter is from nonhuman earthly forms. His reading in the history of philosophy made Novalis familiar with Platonic ideas, and like others of his generation such as Hegel and the poet Hölderlin, he is able to reconcile these with Christian conceptions of spirituality. The realm of spirit, the repository of truth, is conceived as the end of all philosophical and creative thought, but Novalis sees the way of its attainment in something other than a search for heterogeneous new discoveries. It is accessible only through perfect self-understanding, which for him is the beginning of all knowledge and all philosophy.

It is apparent that in these interlocking concepts of pure spirit and self-knowledge, Novalis is positing a kind of truth very different from the belief in objective reason that underlies the assumptions of Enlightenment rationalism. Notwithstanding the continuities that link many aspects of eighteenth-century philosophical thinking to that of Novalis's time, such a departure goes far to justify the traditional periodic differentiation between the Enlightenment and Romanticism. The mystical dimension of his religious upbringing disposed Novalis toward nonrational ways of understanding, a direction that was reinforced by his reading of Hemsterhuis. In arguments that privilege introspection and intuition, Novalis insists on the subjective nature of truth: "but is not the universe *within ourselves*? The depths of our spirit are unknown to us— the mysterious way leads inwards" (MO 17).

Drawing a distinction that clarifies his concept of subjective truth, Novalis writes that we can be convinced only of magical or miraculous truth, never of natural truth (LFI 78). With this distinction he circumvents a correspondence theory of truth that would demand validity in terms of objective reality, and puts in its place a self-generating, poetic truth. This truth is the only truth that is accessible to me, for if I look elsewhere then the only difference between truth and delusion lies in their life functions (MO 8). The idea of magical truth will prove to be central to Novalis's aesthetic principle of magical idealism. His rejection of a notion of extrinsic truth that can be uncovered by the exercise of reason is at one with the stance of contemporary pragmatists. Philosophers like Richard Rorty have argued against the assumptions of an objective theory of truth such as that held in the Enlightenment, as the way of discovering "the intrinsic nature of things."[1] Novalis, in contrast, proposes a self-referential model for philosophy which seeks not to explain the world but rather to explain itself; its growth is organic, as a seed emerges from a husk and sprouts to form a new plant (LFI 17). The image recalls his description of his own fragments as "seedings."

In another sense too, Novalis's ideas come close to those of Rorty and others who move out from a subjective notion of truth to a cohesive sense of participation in a human community. What Rorty calls solidarity or ethnocentricity embodies a kind of social optimism that is close to Novalis's post-Enlightenment belief in progress.[2] If truth is not something to be discovered external to myself, but lies rather in acting according to my convictions (MO 38), it is as much an ethical as an epistemological concept. In this sense, it represents the core of that element of late-eighteenth-century German thought which Novalis shared with his philosophical partners and to which he returns again and again: the social responsibility of the intellectual. The philosopher and the artist are gifted with the ability to recognize magical truth, and are therefore called on to guide others toward this recognition: "We are on a *mission*. Our vocation is the education of the earth" (MO 32). The political and social aspirations derived from the belief in progress will be examined more closely in connection with Novalis's writing on the poetic state, in *Faith and Love or The King and Queen* and *Christendom or Europe*.

Recognition of social responsibility precludes the escapism or narcissism that have sometimes been held to inform Novalis's ideas. Indeed, it is precisely the act of distancing from the self that he characterizes as the highest task of education: ". . . to take command of one's transcendental self—to be at once the I of its I" (MO 28). As part of his intensive study of Fichte during 1796, Novalis had set out to redefine the relation between the intuitive and cognitive functions of the self, between feeling and reflection, content and form. Through an interactive process that Novalis calls *ordo inversus*, as the self reaches consciousness of itself these two functions come together, subject and object becoming one. This insight underlies Novalis's theory of representation and his vision of the practice of philosophy as art.

As a creative dynamic, the concept of potentiation or reflection, exemplified in the phrase "the I of its I," is at the heart of Romantic aesthetics. It is defined by Friedrich Schlegel in terms such as poetry of poetry and philosophy of philosophy, signifying a continuous progression of ever greater intensity and power. But for Novalis the reflection formula has more than purely intellectual force; the *ordo inversus* is infused with a characteristic sense of mystical understanding. He embraces the common goals of the Schlegel circle but endows them with a larger dimension: "The world must be made Romantic. . . . To make Romantic is nothing but a qualitative raising to a higher power" (LFI 66). Raising the self to the power of itself is perhaps the most consequential of all the Romantic reflection formulas, since it describes a progressive mental act whereby, in perfect self-knowledge, one's gaze is simultaneously extricated from the bounds of individuality. Not forgetful absorption in the self but the converse, critical contemplation, is the goal: "As we behold ourselves—we give ourselves life" (MO 102). Through the *feeling* of the self *reflecting* on itself, transcendent or magical truth may be revealed.

The coinage "logological" shows a new application of the reflection formula. The notebooks that complement *Miscellaneous Observations* are concerned for the most part with different aspects of philosophy in the past, present, and future. Novalis defines his own practice as "logological," meaning the activity of logic raised to the power of itself or reflecting on its own nature, where "logic" is used in a nontechnical sense to equate "philosophical discourse." "Logology," therefore, is the process of self-conscious reflection on the practice of philosophy, the word itself implying a progressive movement or growth toward a new, higher stage. Novalis restates the grounding principles of his thought: that philosophy is possible at all derives from the ability of the intelligence to act on itself (LFI 22). Philosophy begins with the act of transcending the self (LFI 79).

In a retrospective glance at the evolution of philosophy, Novalis does not undertake a review of historical figures in "lexicographical" or "philological" fashion, a method he will later deplore (TF 34). It is rather a kind of typology of the organic growth that he describes elsewhere in the metaphor of the seed and the plant. Late-eighteenth-century notions of human progress commonly adopted a triadic pattern, seeing in it evolution from a primitive or chaotic phase through a stage of searching and experimentation toward ultimate resolution. Novalis employs this pattern as he traces three phases of philosophy passing through a process of growth and change (LFI 13). None is identified with a specific historical period, although the third and last may be assumed to be Novalis's own time or, more properly, the age that was about to dawn. He and his fellow Romantics were conscious of the symbolism of the new century, an awareness that informs much of their writing on history, politics, and culture.

Novalis's brief overview culminates in a presaging of the philosophy of the new age, when rational argument and intuition will come together in an all-embracing kind of philosophy that is also art. It is the artist who will achieve a necessary synthesis both within himself and, through contemplation of himself, in his vision of the transcendental: "The complete representation of true spiritual life, raised to consciousness through this action, is *philosophy kat exochen*." The universe of the spiritual or of magical truth reflected in art becomes "the kernel or germ of an all-encompassing organism—It is the beginning of a true *self-penetration of the spirit* which never ends." That art should be perceived as the ultimate phase of philosophy shows Novalis moving radically in the direction of bringing together all dimensions of intellectual life into a whole that is grounded in representation. This vision is guided by the idea of the *ordo inversus*, whereby subject becomes object, self becomes nonself, the symbol becomes the symbolized, and philosophy becomes poetry. The key to these transformations is found in language, the primary site of representation.

The later eighteenth century was a time of much speculation on the origin and nature of language. Rousseau, Herder, and many others differentiated human speech from the articulations of animals by reference to the concept of "instinct," which was believed to be weak in human beings in comparison with animals. It was therefore held that language must be a function of reason, something other than instinct, and arrived at by imitation and analogy. When we read what Novalis has to say about language, however, it is arresting to find a different position that is much closer to theories widely accepted today. *Miscellaneous Observations* and the *Logological Fragments* as well as the *Monologue*, a short essay on language, include many passages that show that Novalis believed language to be an innate quality of the mind and that human beings possess the instinct to speak.[3]

In line with his principle of self-knowledge as the essential first step toward philosophy, Novalis focuses on the mental capacity that is the prerequisite of knowledge: "How can a person have a sense of something if he does not have the germ of it within himself. What I am to understand must develop organically within me" (MO 19). Elsewhere he speaks explicitly of an organ of thought comparable with the eye or the ear, and of ordinary communication as the "product of the higher organ of language" (LFII 19, 36). Language is "a product of the organic drive for development. . . . It has a positive, free origin" (LFI 83).[4] Just as the innateness hypothesis has led many modern linguists to move away from the belief that language is culturally determined, Novalis argues against the notion that language arises as a result of sense impressions, defining it rather as a system of nonsensory or immediate knowledge: "All sense perception is at secondhand" (LFI 72).

Seeking to identify the mental processes involved in the attainment of language, Novalis distinguishes between what he calls the mechanics and the dynamics of thinking (LFI 15). The mechanics of thinking he designates as "the grammar of higher language or thought" or as "common logic," a term that in this context ought not to be equated with the root or factor of "logology," that is, as philosophical discourse in a general sense, but rather as a mental function. The idea of a grammar or logic of higher language, a "physiology of concepts," is very close to the Chomskian theory of universal grammar, the "organ" that underlies all human language. Within the innate structures of thinking, Novalis continues, a dynamics is produced, which he calls "metaphysics," which has to do with "original mental powers." These powers are the productive or generative aspect of thinking, "the soul of the philosophy of mind." Novalis has arrived at a position espoused by Steven Pinker and other Chomskians, who hold that we think in a special language of thought or mentalese, in which there are many more concepts than words.[5] "How often one feels the poverty of words," Novalis remarks, "to express several ideas all at once" (MO 70). "Words are a deceptive medium for what is already thought" (LFI 3).

Nonetheless, language provides the fabric from which we fashion our intuited sense of things. For the philosopher-artist, language's power of symbolization provides an essential tool. As we have seen, Novalis is prepared to accept that there is no objective form of truth but only that which we arrive at by introspection and feeling: "All cognition, knowledge etc. may well be reduced to comparisons, resemblances" (LFI 68). Through the working of the *ordo inversus*, our intuitive perception of objects and ideas is transformed into cognition as we distinguish them by name. Naming is perhaps the first and the simplest form of symbolization; once a name is established, it takes on a functional value of its own, giving form to our intuited understanding. Using cosmological imagery that is complementary to his customary seeding metaphor, Novalis marvels at the insight derived from this moment of language made conscious in naming: "How easy is it then to make use of the universe! how visible is the concentricity of the spiritual world!" (MO 2). Intuition and cognition are bound together in a kind of hermeneutic circle, so that all we perceive and understand is held in a centripetal relationship, each element illuminating the whole and being illuminated by it. The argument is summed up aphoristically: "Several names are of benefit to an idea" (MO 36).

The symbolic function of language takes on particular significance for Novalis, given his belief in the validity of mystical understanding and its admission to the discourse of philosophy. From his study of Hemsterhuis, Novalis adopted the idea that all knowledge must be articulated poetically, and he stresses the cognitive aspect of poetic thinking in many contexts. With many of his contemporaries he recognized the supreme achievement of Fichte as the creation of a new kind of language that made it possible for philosophical writing to become poetic. His aspiration to emulate or to surpass Fichte in this respect led him to write of the need for a special "language of tropes and riddles" to be used for initiates (FL 1), but more persuasively he demonstrated its principles in the figurative and rhetorical style of his own language.

The short essay known as the *Monologue* celebrates the mysterious working of intuitive language, relating it to magical truth. This truth is uncovered by introspection but also through the spontaneous and generative power of a language that is conscious only of itself. Such inner language is close to song in that it is produced or modulated without choice or intention, like sensation or consciousness itself (cf. TF 47). It becomes poetry in its ability to construct the transcendental or magical world in the language of symbols (LFI 42). In the *Monologue* Novalis compares language to mathematics, finding the essence of each in their autonomous character, since they relate in their generative structure purely to themselves and not to anything external. But language is endowed with the power of symbolization that allows it to create for us an image of the world.

In his conception of the new art of philosophy as a kind of world-making, Novalis demonstrates how far he has come from the idea of art as mimesis. More than once he makes explicit that the doctrine of imitation in the arts must be overcome: "Poetry too must simply be merely sensible — *artificial — invented*. . . . Even in the theatre the principle of imitation of nature still tyrannizes" (LaF 45). In this respect he may be seen to share in the turning away from the aesthetics of mimesis that pervades the last third of the eighteenth century. But neither does he accept the expressivist theory that for many was the successor to the doctrine of mimesis. As may be expected from his observations on the creative activity of language in shaping its own world, Novalis conceives of poetry, the highest form of all language, as something that creates rather than imitates, that speaks rather than expresses anything extrinsic, even the thoughts or feelings of its originator.

The assumption of autonomy in poetic and philosophical discourse underlies all his discussion of the nature of representation in metaphor, image, and symbol. Once more Novalis anticipates contemporary views on the language and the metaphorical function of art. Nelson Goodman has argued that the arts neither depict nor express anything in the life-world. Rather, they refer metaphorically to the world by possessing certain features of it within their own symbolic system.[6] The coherence of any art work, that which makes it intelligible, does not derive from extrinsic factors made present by imitation or expression. It stems from the autonomous meaning constructed within its symbolic system and the particular "voice" that allows its symbolism to be articulated. Goodman's theory of metaphorical reference in art is analogous to Rorty's rejection of the correspondence theory of truth in favor of one that posits a self-contained cognitive world. For Novalis, just as magical truth is not a reflection of something extrinsic to the self but rather is constructed by the self in contemplation of itself, so art is not imitation of external reality but a new world made by its own autonomous activity.

In applying his theory of the autonomy of art to particular literary forms, Novalis distinguishes between artificial and natural or artless poetry. If poetry, on the one hand, at a less perfect stage of its development betrays a specific purpose, as allegory or rhetoric may do, then it remains for Novalis in the category of artificial poetry (LFII 15), where representation is subjugated to the explicit purpose of communication. Natural poetry, on the other hand, is free, undetermined, and immediate, directly combining communication and representation as the language of hiero-glyphs once did. For Novalis as for his colleagues of the Romantic school, the novel, a kind of narrative that had become established only in the last generation in Germany, was the literary form par excellence. Novalis adapts Friedrich Schlegel's theory of the novel as a progressive, universal form for the modern age in his own terminology. The novel, paradigm of natural poetry, is not constrained by the demands of imitation, expres-sion, or formal tradition; it is free to grow organically as philosophy does. In illustration of the formula of potentiation, Novalis writes that the novel grows in a movement of geometrical progression (LFI 28). But besides the novel Novalis seeks to bring many other kinds of narrative into his def-inition of natural poetry.

A section of his notebooks headed "Anecdotes" (LFII 11–16) con-tains a discussion of story telling as a way of representing magical truth. His emphasis here is not on the novel or any modern narrative ("The world of books is indeed only a caricature of the real world" LFII 20), but on a form of poetry yet to be achieved. The purely poetic anecdote, a story that refers only to itself (LFII 12), will signal the attainment of a new, higher phase of art through the poeticization of the present world. Presaging some of the genres of later European Romanticism, Novalis evokes symbolic or prelinguistic narratives such as are found in dream, myth, magic, or fairy tale (cf. MO 100). These are the models for his own fiction in *The Apprentices at Saïs* and *Heinrich von Ofterdingen*. In exploring the cognitive aspect of symbolic poetic forms, Novalis begins to open up a theory of representation that is central to his conception of poetic truth.

In his exploration of what it is to be human, Novalis refers to a higher realm of spirit, or magical truth. Only in relation to this realm does the human being acquire meaning. Asking what a human being is, Novalis finds an answer in a rhetorical figure: "A perfect trope of the spirit" (LFII 5). In another part of the notebooks the same idea of metaphor is extended: "The world is a *universal trope* of the spirit—a sym-bolic picture of it" (TF 25). These profound and puzzling ideas are fur-ther pursued in entries in his *General Draft* for an encyclopedia, under the keywords "cosmology" and "psychology." Cosmological thinking for Novalis has to do with our perception of the world and our interaction with it. But the notion of human being and world as metaphors of the spirit touches more intimately on the question of how we perceive and feel the relations between all three; it is a psychological question. Under this head, Novalis argues that to understand anything we need to see it represented, however much the character of its representation at first seems paradoxical (GD 1).

Novalis has made clear that the dynamic of language as of art is not imitation but a spontaneous, intuitive movement. Representation, as a function of mind, is for him equally far from the imitation of anything observed or conceived a priori. "All representation," he writes (GD 40), "rests on making present that which is not present." His examples are the ideals or hypotheses that he refers to elsewhere as cultural goals: eternal peace or the golden age, for instance. When we explain what we mean by these we construct an image of them so that the listener or reader can grasp their nature. Representation then becomes a kind of implied "conversation," in the sense of Richard Rorty, in that "making present that which is not present" sets up a series of questions and answers to consider its character and the possibility of its realization.[7] In this way, for example, self and nonself each represent the other and can thereby approach both mutual and self-understanding (GD 1).

His theory of mutual representation allows Novalis to assert the paradoxical identity of self and nonself (LFI 59). He describes this insight as "the highest principle of all *learning* and *art*," and writes: "It is *all one* whether I posit the universe in myself or myself in the universe" (GD 31), since the presence of one will simultaneously make metaphorically present the other that was absent. These paradoxes are reminiscent of Hegel's idea of *Verrücktheit* (madness or disruption), whereby consciousness becomes capable of escaping from the limitations of self, an indispensable first step toward discovery of the language of the spirit.[8] But it is not to be forgotten that Novalis is himself using the language of tropes in making these statements. They are rhetorical stratagems designed to set up a conversation in his own mind and in that of the reader.

In a veritably Derridean deferral of closure, undermining any literal acceptance of a theory of representation, he remarks that every symbol has its countersymbol. The image and the original are never identical, no matter how close the resemblance; representation is never complete (GD 36). So the open-endedness of his philosophical discourse is demonstrated at the very moment when Novalis is expounding its central idea. It is significant that the entry where he notes, without further comment: "Theory of the *mutual representation of the universe*," is under the keyword "Magic" (GD 12). The realm of magic occupies a pivotal place for

Novalis both conceptually and in his poetic work, but these insights do not prevent him from exploring more practical and even mundane areas of inquiry, among them social life, science, and politics.

Novalis once commented that the distractions of ordinary life inhibit "the higher development of our nature. Divinatory, magical, truly poetic people cannot come into being under circumstances such as ours" (LFI 27). A visit to the spa resort of Teplitz in the summer of 1798, however, finds him seeking to apply philosophical thinking to the affairs of the world. The new direction is marked with the comment: "Notes in the margin of life." A series of entries touch on everyday things—foods, illness, the relations between men and women, the role of religion in society. In a letter to Friedrich Schlegel, Novalis describes his philosophy of everyday life as "moral astronomy in the sense of Hemsterhuis." The metaphor emphasizes the importance of centripetal social mechanisms and the communal obligations within them, exemplified by the practices of religion.

Elsewhere he acknowledges the need for a mediator in the practice of religion (MO 73), and for the Christian, the supreme form of mediation is found in the symbolic commemorative meal of the Eucharist with its sacrificial reference. Many layers of meaning are suggested by the Eucharist in the light of Novalis's theory of mutual representation. The physical consumption of the Eucharist is a metaphor for the spiritual partaking of the divine, when the absent body of Christ is made present. Reflecting on the blending of physical and spiritual substance embodied in the sacrament, Novalis sees it as something like an embrace, an exchange of love (TF 1), and Christ therefore as *the key to the world* (TF 36). But Novalis draws a further parallel between the significance of the Eucharist and the consumption of ordinary food in the company of friends. We depend on the natural world for survival, yet we depend as much for spiritual food on friendship and the company of those we love. Eating becomes a trope where body is substituted for spirit (TF 11).

In writing of the love between men and women, Novalis begins with the simple note "Sofie, or on women" (TF 15). In March 1797, Novalis's first fiancée, Sophie von Kühn, died at the age of fifteen. Her name retained something like religious significance for him. It symbolizes love and womanhood, but it also represents philosophy, the pursuit of which, since his engagement to Sophie, was infused in his mind with the idea of love. He describes philosophy as like a caress (LFI 12) or a first kiss (LFI 57). The kind of poetic philosophy to which Novalis aspires, and that is both the end and the means of Romanticizing the world, is an all-embracing, creative activity, comparable only to love, "the *unum* of the universe" (GD 2). In social terms, marriage and the family represented for Novalis the immediate context of love, centering on a woman as wife and mother.

In respect of matters having significant personal or emotional content Novalis appears more constrained by historical context than in addressing abstract questions of metaphysics or epistemology. To a modern reader, his reflections on women betray an essentialist point of view that seems little enlightened by his unprejudiced and even progressive attitudes on issues such as politics and the state. Using an analogy that objectifies women and denies them any real intellectuality, Novalis remarks that they are "similar to the infinite in that they cannot be squared" (TF 17). This is as much as to say that women are incapable of self-knowledge, the beginning of all philosophy, which is attained by raising the self to the power of itself. Women are inert: sometimes idle and helpless like children, sometimes remote and inspiring like higher beings. Like nature, they are present yet ineluctable, mysterious yet ordinary. Only in respect of the capacity to love does Novalis acknowledge the moral strength of women to be very great.

The analogy drawn here between women and nature suggests that Novalis might conceive the natural world also not as open to definitive analysis or description, as Enlightenment science had assumed, but only to hypothesis. We are today accustomed to questioning the objectivity of scientific truth as much as any defined within the area of metaphysics, but it is perhaps inappropriately consequential that we should look for such approaches in Novalis. In his observations on the natural sciences, Novalis rarely asks questions that would match those he poses in regard to philosophical truth. He draws clear distinctions between science and philosophy, asserting that the former is determinate while the latter is indeterminate (LFII 31); philosophy is not concrete as are mathematics and physics (GD 34). Mechanical causation, something with which the mining engineer Friedrich von Hardenberg was obliged to be familiar, is "unnatural to the spirit" (LFII 17). Yet Novalis maintained that all learning must become one (MO 4, LaF 39), envisioning a blending of knowledges in a universal formation of individual and community. In this desire to incorporate the natural sciences into a seamless study of knowledge Novalis is at his most characteristic.

Soon after the Teplitz visit, Novalis began the series of notebooks that he called his *General Draft* for an encyclopedia. It ranges over philosophy and religion, science and mathematics, politics, literature and the arts, sexuality and psychology. A selection designed to give some idea of the scope of the encyclopedic project is translated here. The theoretical perspectives opened up in the *General Draft*, on which he worked throughout the winter of 1798–1799, show the impact of his professional scientific activities and his literary plans, as well as the published work of his Romantic colleagues and conversations with them. An example of this cross-fertilization is his response to Friedrich Schlegel's review of Goethe's novel *Wilhelm Meister's Apprenticeship*. The review, published in July 1798, prompted Novalis to further reflection on the novel and other types of narrative, but it also led him to consider Goethe's work in a quite new way.

In his short essay on Goethe, his only extended piece of criticism, he discusses the latter's scientific essays together with his fiction. He sees Goethe's study of botany and optics as complementary to his creative writing. Conversely, his way of contemplating nature as an artist means "in a certain sense that Goethe is the first physicist of his age." In either field, his supreme powers of representation lift his work to the level of applied philosophy. Novalis perceives Goethe's achievement as an example of what he advocates as the coming phase of philosophy, in this case natural philosophy, as art. In the manuscripts the Goethe essay is followed by a series of entries on various scientific, medical, and literary topics, somewhat in the style of the *General Draft*, which he was about to begin. They are complemented by a number of observations on painting and sculpture, prompted by a visit to the Dresden Gallery in the company of other members of the Schlegel group.

The Gallery housed one of the finest collections in Europe, including Raphael's Sistine Madonna, many fine Dutch and Italian landscapes, and an impressive set of plaster reproductions of Greek sculptures. Novalis's notebooks at this time record how the collection provided "a storeroom of indirect stimuli of all kinds for the poet" (OG 26). Typically his observations take him away from particular examples to new theoretical positions. Landscape painting leads him to reflect on the chemistry, botany, and geology of natural landscape, thus pursuing the kind of organic reasoning ("*thinking* in the *body*" OG 25) that he praised in Goethe. The antiquities prompt more far-reaching questions on our perception of history and the possibility of progress.

In this context Novalis demonstrates that his thinking about science and nature is embryonically as open to reconsideration as his more articulated ideas on truth and representation. In the Goethe essay he draws an inspired comparison between our informed contemplation or, in modern terminology, our construction of antiquity and a possible way of contemplating nature that is modern and specific to our time: "Nature and insight into nature come into being at the same time, like antiquity and the knowledge of antiquities." Neither "antiquity" nor "nature" exist as concepts until the modern mind constructs them as such. Just as truth is not something to be discovered but something made by us, so the world of history and the natural world have first to be perceived as entities accessible to our understanding before they can be said to exist conceptually. This incipient questioning of the assumptions of science as an objective study of nature remains undeveloped. But it is tempting to speculate that, had Novalis lived longer, he may have interrogated the premises of scientific inquiry with the same blend of skepticism and passion he brought to philosophy.

Much of the last two years of Novalis's life was devoted to professional work and to creative writing. But he continued to work on his philosophical and scientific notebooks, and also completed the essay *Christendom or Europe*. In the decade after the French Revolution, debate on the desirable form of the state continued in Germany as elsewhere in Europe. For Novalis, that form could only be one that embodied the ideal of Romanticization; the poetic state was to be the state of the future, just as philosophy and all forms of knowledge were to become poetic. Political observations are scattered throughout the unpublished manuscripts, and Novalis had already achieved a degree of notoriety as a political thinker with his second published collection of fragments, *Faith and Love or The King and Queen*, which appeared in July 1798 in the Berlin journal *Yearbooks of the Prussian Monarchy*.

King Frederick William III and Queen Luise of Prussia ascended the throne at the end of 1797. Unlike their predecessors, they were known for their domestic and familial virtue, so providing Novalis with the perfect symbolism to clothe his ideas on monarchy and the poetic state. There is no question of his legitimist views, but as in all other fields, Novalis's political attitudes take some unexpected turns, and in any case they are directed less toward present circumstances than toward a future ideal. He sees the royal family above all as a model for the society of which it is the pinnacle, while the queen is the inspiration for the king to fulfil his own role (FL 24). Novalis's idealization of the figure of the queen undoubtedly owes much to the real person of the youthful, upright, and gracious Queen Luise, but his portrait is primarily a stylized image of the place of love in the ideal society. If *faith* in the monarchy as the only form of government is essential for the poetic state, it is equally indispensable that *love* be recognized as the element that binds all the members of the state together.

Consistent with most later eighteenth-century writers on the political form of the state, Novalis sees no contradiction between a monarchy and republican government, but rather maintains that king and republic can only exist with each other (FL 22). A republic constitutes that kind of government where the people, or their representatives, have some share in the affairs of state. But for Novalis the monarch is the linchpin in the symbolic hierarchy that constitutes the national community. The king is therefore the true representation of the res publica, given the literal meaning of the republic as the public good. Democracy is posited as the equivalent of monarchy where the latter represents the total will of the people (MO 122). Institutional democracy, which rests on the decisions of the majority, is likely to be something imperfect, very different from the symbolic, aesthetic kind embodied in the monarch, who is the natural exemplar of his people in a way no elected representative can be. True democracy can be found where "the original laws of humanity" (FL 67) take shape in the most natural way, in the monarchy.

Notwithstanding political judgments in defence of the monarchy, which appear to be inflexibly conservative, Novalis's comments on the Revolution are never wholly negative. His witty observation that Burke had written a revolutionary book against the Revolution (MO 115) points to his critical, rather than condemnatory, attitude toward the possibility of fundamental political change. It is consequent on Novalis's concept of the poetic state that anarchical or negative energy and the loss of a vision of the future should be rejected. However, this is not to say that the productive dynamic of revolutionary action is to be suppressed or denied. Novalis's conservatism is not reactionary but radical, forcing confrontation of the consequences of revolutionary change as much as of those of sanguine acceptance of the status quo. The collection ends with an appeal for tolerance and maturity, which will lead to "the sublime conviction of the relativity of every positive form" (FL 68). It is a conclusion that seems to betray Novalis's distaste for the immediacy of political controversy, but which is also at one with the belief in the fluidity of conceptual thinking he shared with the members of the Schlegel circle and their contemporary Hegel.

Novalis's political essay, *Christendom or Europe*, was written in October 1799 under the immediate influence of Schleiermacher's *Speeches on Religion*. At first reading, *Christendom or Europe* appears to be a work in praise of medieval Catholic Christendom. It has often been cited as evidence of a reactionary tendency to be found in Novalis himself and that is perceived as characteristic of German Romanticism as a whole. While he deplores the divisiveness of the Reformation, Novalis's argument is not directed against change and growth in the religious culture of Europe. "Progressive, ever-expanding evolutions are the stuff of history." He admits the need for the Reformation because of the complacency and materialism that had overtaken the Church, and restrictive measures such as the celibacy of the clergy, but deprecates the schismatic and secular character of Protestantism, particularly its fragmentation in a number of national churches.

Both the Reformation itself and modern philosophy, that is, the French-inspired philosophy of the late eighteenth century, are held by Novalis to be deficient in their pursuit of rational or literal knowledge at the expense of mystery and the supernatural. Protestant emphasis on the Bible rather than tradition and ritual found its eighteenth-century counterpart in a style of learning and education that was fundamentally secular and therefore spiritually sterile. Now, in his own time, Novalis is able to foresee a regeneration of religion out of just that confusion and disorder that he perceives in the modern world as the result of conflicting spiritual and intellectual currents: "True anarchy is the element within which religion is born." It is this turn toward the future that makes *Christendom or Europe* a programmatic work rather than a purely critical one, and that gives the lie to any dismissal of it as reactionary. As in *Faith and Love or The King and Queen*, the assessment of the Revolution here is one of circumspect recognition of its dynamic function in the slow process of change that is the essence of history.

The closing paragraphs of *Christendom or Europe* represent a summation of Novalis's critique of the Enlightenment. He stresses the positive impact of rationalism during the later eighteenth century in providing an extreme position that later thinkers were obliged to counter. But for the domination of reason, the new, productive period that is to come, when poetry will open the door to all the riches of art and nature, would not have been possible. In prophetic mode, Novalis speculates on the possibility of peace and even political union among the European states, arguing dialectically from the upheaval and conflict in Europe in the autumn of 1799. The integration of philosophy and learning in the new golden age can perhaps be matched by the political integration of the states of Europe, if the present wars can be turned to good account and a sense of wholeness revived. What had seemed a nostalgic rhapsody in praise of the unity of medieval Christendom now appears as a symbolic argument positing an ideally harmonious world in political as well as philosophical terms. A vision of the new Jerusalem, presented at the end of the essay, becomes the crowning image of Novalis's hope for the future of Germany and Europe, as it would be in Blake's vision for England a few years later.

Novalis proposes a reconciliation of seemingly disparate ways of appropriating the world. In the practices of art, philosophy, science, and religion we seek to understand ourselves and our place in the world, but if the golden age is to be realized then these discourses must flow together. Within the tendency of his time toward breaking down the barriers between reason and the imagination, Novalis shared in the intellectual ecumenism of Friedrich Schlegel and the synthesizing dynamic of the young Hegel. But his valorization of intuitive thinking brought an additional dimension to his philosophical practice. This quality is best elucidated in his idea of magic as something both liberating and fructifying.

Magic is defined by Novalis in a number of complementary ways. For the individual it is "the art of using the world of the senses at will" (LFI 69), whereby the body is transcended by the spirit. Although he does not employ religious terminology, the parallels to the pietist and mystical thought that shaped his early education are clear. He compares enthusiasm (in the eighteenth-century sense of being filled with God) to a kind of madness "governed by rules and in full consciousness," and continues: "Communal madness ceases to be madness and becomes magic" (LFI 70). If a community so wills, it can transcend the boundaries of the rational and move into a higher realm of experience. "Magic" takes on the character of a universal transformation defined elsewhere by Novalis as "the Romanticization of the world." All learning can be animated by this transformation, for example in "magical chemistry, mechanics, and physics" (GD 2), "magical astronomy, grammar, philosophy, religion" (GD 12).

While logology is defined as philosophical discourse raised to the power of itself, it implies still the practice of philosophy in an expert sense, informed by argument and precedent. As against this, magical philosophy is a way of constructing a worldview independently of extrinsic knowledge, much as language arises innately and independently of sensory knowledge. It is a creative act indistinguishable in essence from art. As the supreme human task, it has its foundation in love, which makes all magic possible (GD 7). The resolution of difference, including that between self and other, lies in the free activity of the imagination outside the laws of causation. Then "philosophy appears here entirely as magical idealism" (GD 43). This last explanation is probably the closest we have to a definition of "magical idealism." It is the philosophy of the future that is also art, magical in that it transcends causation and the senses, ideal since it belongs in the realm of pure spirit to which we aspire. Magical idealism becomes both an artistic and a philosophical principle, making magical truth present in all discourse.

In the notebooks compiled between the spring of 1799 and late autumn 1800, before illness prevented him from continuing them, Novalis turns most often to consideration of poetry and other literary forms. He has much to say about the novel, both in criticism of Goethe's *Wilhelm Meister's Apprenticeship* and in evocation of very different narrative styles such as fairy tale. These preoccupations reflect his current work on his own poetic novel *Heinrich von Ofterdingen*, itself an attempt to demonstrate the fusion of prose narrative and poetry. In more theoretical reflections, the poet is compared to a religious prophet in that he has the gift of *speaking* the world of magical philosophy where all exists without cause, "like the sounds of the Aeolian harp" (LaF 1, 42). His world is constructed purely through the exercise of his imagination, as in other transcending states such as mysticism or madness: "The poet is truly bereft of his senses—instead everything takes place within him. In the truest sense he presents *subject object—mind and world*" (LaF 40).

It was the destiny of Novalis's generation that many died in youth, as he himself did a few weeks before his twenty-ninth birthday. His *Hymns to the Night*, written early in 1800, are a poetic meditation on the mystery of death. In his philosophical fragments Novalis speaks of death positively, seeing it as the ultimate form of transcending the self that is necessary for philosophy to begin, "a victory over the self" (MO 11). Life and death are perceived as two elements of an equation that expresses the coherence of our existence: "Death is at once the end and the beginning—at once separation and closer union of the self. Through death the reduction is complete" (MO 15). In an observation that adds existential force to his characterization of magical idealism, Novalis defines death as "the Romanticizing principle of our life" (LaF 5). If death, like love, can be construed as that which lends meaning to life, then it signifies freedom from contingency and causation. The way to magical philosophy is open.

There is an exhilarating vigor in Novalis's philosophical writings that stems from their disconcerting heterogeneity as well as their refusal to be bound by established categories. The reader is made aware of an intellectual optimism that pervades all his work, a conviction that the universal synthesis that it envisions can be achieved. Lent impetus by his belief in perfectibility, this conviction explains the engaging sense of being at the threshold of new discovery that underlies all his writing. Novalis can be seen as a thinker who points forward to the new century with its massive social and scientific change, and to kinds of innovation in intellectual and artistic fields that he could not have foreseen, but that are implicit in the open-endedness of his thought.

1 *Miscellaneous Observations*

1. We *seek* the absolute everywhere and only ever *find* things.[1]

2. Signifying by sounds and marks is an admirable abstraction.[2] Three letters signify God for me—a few marks signify a million things. How easy it is then to make use of the universe! how visible is the concentricity of the spiritual world! The theory of language is the dynamic of the spiritual realm! One word of command moves armies—the word liberty—nations.

3. The world state is the body which is—animated by the world of beauty, the world of sociability. It is the necessary instrument of this world.

4. Apprenticeship suits the novice poet—academic study the novice philosopher.
The academy ought to be a thoroughly philosophical institution—only one faculty—the whole establishment organized—to arouse and exercise the *power of the mind* in a purposive way.
The best kind of apprenticeship is apprenticeship in the art of living. Through carefully planned experiments one becomes familiar with its principles and acquires the skill to act according to them as one wishes.

5. The spirit is perpetually proving itself.

6. We shall never entirely comprehend ourselves, but we will and can do much more than comprehend ourselves.

7.   Certain *restraints* are like the finger positions of a flute-player, who stops now this hole and now that in order to produce different sounds, but *seems* to be making *random* combinations of silent and speaking holes.

8.   The distinction between delusion and truth lies in the difference in their life functions.
Delusion lives on truth—truth bears its life within itself. We destroy delusion as we destroy illnesses—and thus delusion is nothing but logical inflammation or its extinction—enthusiasm or Philistinism. The former usually leaves behind—an *apparent lack of mental power*, which can only be redressed by a diminishing series of stimuli (coercive measures). The latter often turns into *deceptive vitality*, whose dangerous revolutionary symptoms can only be relieved by an expanding series of violent measures. Both these dispositions can only be changed by the regular use of strictly followed treatment.

9.   Our entire faculty of perception is like the eye. Objects must pass through opposite mediums in order to appear correctly on the pupil.

10.   Experience is the test of the rational—and vice versa.
The inadequacy of *pure* theory in its application, which is often commented upon by the practician—is found conversely in the rational application of *pure* experience. The true philosopher observes this clearly enough, however he does so while conceding the necessity of this result. For this reason the practician rejects pure theory outright, without realizing how problematic the answer to this question might be.
Does theory exist for the sake of application, or application for the sake of theory?

11.   Death is a victory over the self—which, like all self-conquest, brings about a new, easier existence.

12.   Do we perhaps need so much energy and effort for ordinary and common things because for an authentic human being nothing is more out of the ordinary—nothing more uncommon than wretched ordinariness?
What is highest is the most understandable—what is nearest, the most indispensable. It is only through lack of acquaintance with ourselves— becoming no longer accustomed to ourselves, that a kind of incomprehensibility arises that is itself incomprehensible.

13.   Miracles alternate with the effects of natural laws—they each limit the other, and together they constitute a whole. They are united in that

they complement each other. There is no miracle without a natural event and vice versa.

14.   Nature is the enemy of eternal possessions. It destroys all signs of property according to fixed laws, it eradicates all marks of formation. The earth belongs to all generations—each person has a claim to everything. Those born earlier may owe no advantage to the chance of primogeniture. The right to property is extinguished at certain times. The process of amelioration and deterioration is governed by immutable conditions. But if the body is a property whereby I acquire only the rights of an active citizen of the world, I cannot suffer the loss of myself through loss of this property—I lose nothing but my place in this school for princes—and enter a higher corporate body whither my beloved fellow pupils follow me.

15.   Life is the beginning of death. Life is for the sake of death. Death is at once the end and the beginning—at once separation and closer union of the self. Through death the reduction is complete.

16.   We are close to waking when we dream that we are dreaming.[3]

17.   The imagination places the world of the future either far above us, or far below, or in a relation of metempsychosis to ourselves. We dream of traveling through the universe—but is not the universe *within ourselves*? The depths of our spirit are unknown to us—the mysterious way leads inwards. Eternity with its worlds—the past and future—is in ourselves or nowhere. The external world is the world of shadows—it throws its shadow into the realm of light. At present this realm certainly seems to us so dark inside, lonely, shapeless. But how entirely different it will seem to us—when this gloom is past, and the body of shadows has moved away. We will experience greater enjoyment than ever, for our spirit has been deprived.

18.   Darwin makes the observation that we are less dazzled by the light on waking—if we have been dreaming of visible objects. How fortunate are they, then, who in this life were already dreaming of seeing—they will all the sooner be able to support the glory of the other world!

19.   How can a person have a sense of something if he does not have the germ of it within himself. What I am to understand must develop organically within me—and what I seem to learn is only nourishment—stimulation of the organism.

20.   The seat of the soul is the point where the inner and the outer worlds touch. Wherever they penetrate each other—it is there at every point of penetration.

21.   The life of a truly exemplary person must be constantly symbolic. On this premise, would not every death be a death of expiation? To a greater or lesser extent, of course—and could not several very remarkable conclusions be drawn from this?

22.   Whoever seeks will doubt. But genius tells so boldly and surely what it sees to be happening within itself because it is not hampered in the representation of this, and therefore the representation is not hampered either, but rather its act of contemplation and that which is contemplated seem to be freely in accord, to combine freely in one work.
When we speak of the external world, when we depict real objects, then we are acting as genius does. Thus genius is the ability to treat imaginary objects like real ones, and to deal with them as if they were real as well. Thus the talent of representing, of making an exact observation—of describing the observation purposively—is different from genius. Without this talent one can only half-see—and is only half a genius—one can have gifts of genius which in the absence of that talent are never developed.
None of us would exist at all without the quality of genius. Genius is necessary for everything. But what we usually call genius—is the genius of genius.

23.   It is the most capricious prejudice to believe that a human being is denied the capacity to be *outside himself,* to be consciously beyond the senses. He is capable at any moment of being a suprasensual being. Without this he would not be a citizen of the world—he would be an animal. It is true that under these circumstances reflection, the discovery of oneself—is very difficult, since they are so ceaselessly, so necessarily connected with the change in our other circumstances. But the more conscious of these circumstances we can be, the more lively, powerful, and ample is the conviction which derives from them—the belief in true revelations of the spirit. It is not seeing—hearing—feeling—it is a combination of all three—more than all three—a sensation of immediate certainty—a view of my truest, most actual life—thoughts change into laws—wishes are fulfilled. For the weak person the *fact of this moment is an article of faith.*

The phenomenon becomes especially striking at the sight of many human forms and faces—particularly so on catching sight of many eyes, expressions, movements—on hearing certain words, reading certain passages—at certain views of life, world, and fate. Very many chance incidents, many natural events, particular times of the day and year bring us such experiences. Certain moods are especially favorable to such revelations. Most last only an instant—few linger—fewest of all remain. In this respect there are great differences between people. One is more capable of experiencing revelations than another. One has more *sense* of them, the other more understanding. The latter kind will always remain in their soft light; even if the former has only intermittent flashes of illumination, they are brighter and more varied. This capacity is also susceptible to illness, which signifies either excessive sense and deficient understanding— or excessive understanding and deficient sense.

24.   If a person cannot get any further he finds help in a powerful pronouncement or action—a swift decision.

25.   Shame is probably a feeling of profanation. Friendship, love, and piety ought to be treated with a sense of mystery. One ought to speak about them only in rare, intimate moments, silently agreeing about them. Many things are too delicate to be thought, even more are too much so to be discussed.

26.   Sacrifice of the self is the source of all humiliation, as also on the contrary it is the foundation of all true exaltation. The first step will be an inward gaze—an isolating contemplation of ourselves. Whoever stops here has come only halfway. The second step must be an active outward gaze—autonomous, constant observation of the external world.
No one will ever achieve excellence as an artist who cannot depict anything other than his own experiences, his favorite objects, who cannot bring himself to study assiduously even a quite strange object, which does not interest him at all, and to depict it at leisure. An artist must be able and willing to depict everything. This is how a great artistic style is created, which rightly is so much admired in Goethe.

27.   A remarkable characteristic of Goethe's can be observed in his linking of small, insignificant incidents with more important events. He seems not to harbor any other intention than to engage the imagination in a poetic way with a mysterious kind of game. Here too this extraordinary man has fathomed the secrets of nature and learned a nice artistic knack

thereby.[4] Ordinary life is full of similar incidents. They make up a game which, like all games, ends in both surprise and deception.

Several myths of common life rest on the observation of this upside-down connection—so for instance, *bad dreams* mean good fortune—rumours of one's death mean long life—a hare running across the path means ill fortune. Almost all the superstition of the common people rests on interpretations of this game.

28.   The highest task of education is—to take command of one's transcendental self—to be at once the I of its I. It is all the less to be wondered at that we lack complete insight and understanding for others. Without perfect self-understanding one will never learn to truly understand others.

29.   I show that I have understood a writer only when I can act in his spirit, when, without constricting his individuality, I can translate him and change him in diverse ways.

30.   Humor is a manner that is adopted arbitrarily. The arbitrary is the piquant element in it. Humor is the result of a free mixture of the conditional and the unconditional. Through humor that which is conditional in a particular way becomes interesting in a general way—and acquires objective value. Where imagination and judgment touch, there is wit—where reason and caprice are coupled, there is humor. Persiflage is a kind of humor but ranks one degree lower. It is no longer purely artistic—and much more limited. In serene hearts there is no wit. Wit points to disturbed equilibrium. It is at once the result of the disturbance and the means of restoration. The most powerful wit is found in passion. Truly sociable wit has no bite. There is a kind which is only a magical play of colors in higher spheres. The condition where all relations are dissolved—despair or spiritual death—is the most terrible kind of wit.

Whatever is insignificant, common, rough, ugly, unmannerly, can become socially acceptable *only through wit*. It exists as it were only for the *sake of wit*. What determines its purpose is wit.

31.   That within which the spirit reveals itself ceaselessly is imbued with spirit—or at least where it often reappears in a new or changed form—not merely only once—for instance at the beginning—as in many philosophical systems.

32.   We are on a *mission*. Our vocation is the education of the earth. If a spirit were to appear to us we would at once take control of our own spirituality—we would be inspired through ourselves and the spirit at the

same time. Without inspiration no spirits can appear. Inspiration is appearance and counterappearance, appropriation and communication at the same time.

33.   The human being continues to live and be active only in the realm of ideas—through remembering his existence. At present there is no other way for spirits to be active in this world. Therefore we have a duty to think of the dead. It is the only way to remain in communion with them. God himself cannot be active among us in any other way—than through faith.

34.   Interest is sympathy with the suffering and activity of another being. Something interests me when it is able to arouse my sympathy. No interest is more interesting than that which one takes in oneself—just as the basis of remarkable friendship and love is the sympathy excited in me by a person who is occupied with himself, who through communicating invites me as it were to share in his affairs.

35.   Who can have invented wit? Every characteristic—or mode of conduct of our spirit that is consciously reflected upon is in the truest sense a newly discovered world.

36.   What Schlegel so sharply characterizes as irony is to my way of thinking nothing other—than the result, the character of true reflection—the true presence of the spirit. The spirit appears only in a *strange, airy* form. Schlegel's irony seems to me to be true humor. Several names are of benefit to an idea.[5]

37.   At present spirit is moving only here and there—when will the spirit move in *the whole*? When will humanity en masse itself begin to reflect?

38.   Man has his being in truth—if he sacrifices truth he sacrifices himself. Whoever betrays truth betrays himself. It is not a question of lying—but of acting against one's conviction.

39.   We cannot hear enough or speak enough about an endearing object. We are glad about each new, pertinent, glorifying word. It is not our doing if it does not become the object of all objects.

40.   We cling to lifeless matter because of its connections, its forms. We love matter in so far as it belongs to a beloved being, bears his stamp, or resembles him.

41.   A true club is a mixture of institution and society. It has a purpose, like an institution—not a determinate but an indeterminate one—a free one—humanity as a whole. Every purpose is serious—society is entirely lighthearted.

42.   The objects of social intercourse are nothing *but means to enliven it.* This determines their choice—their variation—their treatment. Society is nothing but *communal living*—one indivisible thinking and feeling person. Each human being is a society in miniature.

43.   To go back into oneself means for us to withdraw from the external world. Analogously, for the spirits earthly life means inward contemplation—going into oneself—immanent action. Thus earthly life springs from an original reflection—a primitive going inward, inner composure—which is as free as our reflection. Conversely spiritual life in this world springs from a breaking through of that primitive reflection. The spirit unfolds itself once more—the spirit goes out to itself again—it cancels that reflection in part—and at this moment it says for the first time—the word *I.* One can see here how relative is the going in and out. What we call going in is actually going out—taking on the original form once again.

44.   Might there not be something to be said for the everyday person, who has recently been so much abused? Does not persistent mediocrity demand the most strength? and is the human being to be more than one of the *popolo*?

45.   Where a genuine propensity to reflection prevails, not merely to thinking this or that thought—there too is *progressivity*.[6] Very many scholars do not possess this propensity. They have learned how to deduce and to infer as a shoemaker learns to make shoes, without its ever having occurred to them or their having taken the trouble to find the basis of their thoughts. However, the way to salvation lies nowhere else. Many people keep this propensity only for a limited period. It grows and dwindles again—very often as the years pass—often with the discovery of a system which they only sought in order to be relieved of the effort of reflection in future.

46.   Error and prejudice are burdens—a means of indirect stimulation for the independent person, the kind who can bear any burden—for the weak they are a means of positive weakening.

47. The people is an idea. We are to become one people. A perfect human being is a people in miniature. True popularity is the highest goal of humanity.

48. Every stage of education begins with childhood. That is why the most educated person on earth so much resembles a child.

49. The transcendental point of view for this life is awaiting us—there we shall find life really interesting for the first time.

50. Every beloved object is the center of a paradise.

51. The interesting is not that which sets me in motion for my own sake, but only as a means, as part of a whole.[7] *The classical* does not disturb me at all—it affects me only indirectly through myself. It does not exist for me, as classical, if I myself do not posit it, as something that would not affect me if I did not determine that I should bring it forth for myself— that would not touch me if I did not tear out a piece of myself and allow this germ to develop in a particular way before my eyes—a development which often needs only a moment—and which coincides with the sense perception of the object—so that I see an object in front of me in which the common object and the ideal, *each permeated by the other*, form only one marvelous whole.

52. To find formulas for individual art objects, whereby they can be understood in the true sense for the first time, constitutes the business of the art critic—whose work is a preparation for the history of art.

53. The more confused a person is—confused people are called block-heads—the more he can make of himself by diligent study of the self. On the other hand, orderly minds must strive to become true scholars—thorough encyclopedists. At first the confused ones must struggle with massive obstacles—they gain insight only *slowly*. They learn to work laboriously—but then they are lords and masters forever. The orderly person swiftly gains insight—but also loses it swiftly. He soon reaches the second stage—but usually he stops there. The last steps are laborious for him, and he can rarely succeed in placing himself in the position of a beginner again once he has attained a certain degree of mastery.
Confusion points to excess of strength and capacity—but deficient equilibrium—precision points to good equilibrium, but meager capacity and strength.

That is why the confused person is so progressive — so perfectible — and why on the other hand the orderly one comes to a halt so early as a Philistine.

To be orderly and precise alone is not to be clear. Through working on himself the confused person arrives at that heavenly transparency — at that self-illumination — which the orderly person so seldom attains.

True genius combines these extremes. It shares swiftness with the last and fullness with the first.

54.   Only the individual is interesting. Hence all that is classical is not individual.[8]

55.   The acuity of genius is the acute use of acuity.

56.   The true letter is of its nature *poetic*.

57.   Wit, as the principle of affinities, is at the same time the *menstruum universale*.[9]

Witty combinations are, for example, Jew and cosmopolitan — childhood and wisdom — brigandage and generosity — virtue and courtesanship — excess and lack of judgment, in naïveté — and so on ad infinitum.

58.   The human being appears at his most worthy when the first impression of him — is the impression of an absolutely witty thought — namely, when he appears to be at once spirit and a particular individual. Every outstanding person must seem to be pervaded by a spirit, as it were, which parodies his visible appearance in the ideal.

In many a person this spirit often shows the visible appearance its backside.

59.   The impulse toward society is the impulse toward organization. Through this spiritual assimilation a good society often arises out of common components around an inspired person.

The interesting is the material which revolves round beauty.

Where there is spirit and beauty, the best of all natures rises high in concentric oscillations.

60.   The German has long been Jack the dullard. But he might indeed soon be the Jack of all Jacks.

It will be with him as with many stupid children — he will live and be clever when his precocious brothers and sisters have long since moldered away, and now he alone is master in the house.

61.   The best thing about learning is its philosophical ingredient—like life in the organic body. If we should dephilosophize learning—what remains—earth, air, and water.

62.   Humanity is a comic role.

63.   Our old nationality, it seems to me, was truly Roman—naturally, because we came into being in just the same way as the Romans—and thus the name Roman Empire would truly be a nice, meaningful coincidence.[10] Germany is Rome, as a country. A country is a great village with its gardens. Perhaps the Capitol could be identified according to the screaming of geese before the Gauls.[11]
The instinctive universal politics and the ambition of the Romans is also found in the German people. The best thing the French have won in the Revolution is a portion of Germanness.[12]

64.   Courts of law, theaters, court, church, government, public meetings—academies, colleges etc. are as it were the special, inner organs of the mystical individual of the state.

65.   All the chance events of our lives are materials from which we can make what we like. Whoever is rich in spirit makes much of his life. Every acquaintance, every incident would be for the thoroughly spiritual person—the first element in an endless series—the beginning of an endless novel.

66.   There are Germans everywhere. The German character is not confined to a particular state, any more than the Roman, the Greek, or the British. They are general human qualities—which have become predominantly general only here and there. Germanness is true popularity and therefore an ideal.

67.   The noble spirit of commerce, truly large-scale trade, only flourished in the Middle Ages and especially at the time of the German Hanseatic League. The Medicis and the Fuggers were proper merchants—our merchants on the whole, not excepting the Hopes and the Teppers, are nothing but grocers.[13]

68.   A translation is either grammatical, or modifying, or mythical.[14] Mythical translations are translations of the highest kind. They represent the pure, perfected character of the individual work of art. They do not give us the real work of art but the ideal of it. There still does not exist, I believe, a complete example of such a translation. But in the spirit of

many a critique and description of works of art clear signs are to be found. A mind is needed where the spirit of poetry and the spirit of philosophy have saturated each other in all their fullness. Greek mythology is in part such a translation of a national religion. The modern Madonna too is such a myth.

Grammatical translations are translations in the usual sense. They require a great deal of learning—but only discursive abilities.

Modifying translations, if they are to be genuine, demand the highest poetic spirit. They easily slip into travesty—like Bürger's Homer in iambics—Pope's Homer—all French translations. The true translator of this kind must indeed be an artist himself and be able to produce the idea of the whole at will in one way or another. He must be the poet of the poet and thus be able to let him speak according to his own and the poet's idea *at the same time.*[15]

The genius of humanity stands in a similar relation to each single person. Not only books but everything can be translated in these three ways.

69.   Sometimes with the most intense pain a paralysis of sensibility occurs. The soul disintegrates—hence the deadly frost—the free power of the mind—the shattering, ceaseless wit of this kind of despair. There is no inclination for anything any more—the person is alone, like a baleful power—as he has no connection with the rest of the world he consumes himself gradually—and in accordance with his own principle he is—misanthropic and *misotheos.*[16] God-hating

70.   Our language is either—mechanical—atomistic—or dynamic. But true poetic language should be organically alive. How often one feels the poverty of words—to express several ideas all at once.

71.   In the state all action is for show—among the people everything is spectacle. The life of the people is a spectacle.
Writings are the thoughts of the state—the archives are its memory.

72.   The more our senses are refined, the more capable they become of distinguishing between individuals. The highest sense would be the highest receptivity to the particularity of human nature. To that would correspond the talent for establishing the nature of the individual, a talent the skill and energy of which are relative. Whenever the will expresses itself in respect of this sense, passions arise for or against individual characteristics—love and hatred.

One owes mastery in playing one's own role to the application of this sense to oneself while reason holds sway.

73.   Nothing is more indispensable for true religious feeling than an intermediary—which connects us to the godhead. The human being is absolutely incapable of sustaining an immediate relation with this. He must be wholly free in the choice of this intermediary. The least compulsion in this matter damages his religion. The choice is distinctive and it follows that educated people will choose rather similar intermediaries—on the other hand that of the uneducated person will in this regard usually be determined by chance. But since so few people are capable at all of a free choice—many an intermediary will become more general—whether by chance—through association, or their particular aptitude for it. This is how national religions arise. The more independent the human being becomes, the more the quantity of the intermediary is diminished, the more the quality is refined—and his relations to it become more diverse and more cultivated—fetishes—stars—animals—heroes—idols—gods— *one* God-man. One soon sees how relative these choices are and one is driven imperceptibly to the idea—that the essence of religion does not in fact depend on the nature of the mediator, but consists purely in the way he is regarded, in the relations that exist with him.

It is idolatry, in a broader sense, if I regard this mediator as in fact God himself. It is *irreligion*, if I accept no mediator at all—and to this extent superstition, or idolatry—and unbelief—or theism, as one could also describe older Judaism—are both *irreligion*. On the other hand atheism is only negation of all religion altogether and thus it has nothing at all to do with religion. True religion is that which accepts that mediator as a mediator—considers him as it were the instrument of the godhead—as its physical appearance. In this respect, at the time of the Babylonian captivity the Jews conceived a genuine religious tendency—a religious hope— faith in a future religion—which radically transformed them in a marvelous way and preserved them with the most remarkable constancy until our time.

But on closer observation, true religion seems once more to be antinomically divided—into pantheism and entheism.[17] I am allowing myself some licence here—in that I am taking pantheism not in the usual sense—but understand by it the idea—that everything could be an instrument of the godhead—could be a mediator, through my raising it to be such—just as entheism on the contrary designates the belief that there is

only one such instrument for us in the world, which alone befits the idea
of a mediator, and through which alone God can be understood—which
I shall thus be compelled to choose through myself—for otherwise entheism would not be true religion.

However incompatible the two seem to be, nonetheless their union can
be effected—if one makes the entheist mediator the mediator of the intermediate world of the pantheist—and as it were centers this by means of
him—so that each makes the other necessary, but in different ways.

Prayer, or religious thought, thus consists in a threefold upwards, indivisible abstraction or positing. Every object can be a temple for the religious
person, in the sense of the augurs. The spirit of this temple is the
omnipresent high priest—the entheistic mediator—who alone stands in
an immediate relation to the All-father.

74.   The basis of all eternal attachment is an absolute tendency in all
directions. On this rests the power of the hierarchy, of true freemasonry,
and the invisible bond of true thinkers—herein lies the possibility of a
universal republic—which the Romans had begun to realize by the time
of the emperors. It was Augustus who first moved away from this basis—
and Hadrian destroyed it altogether.

75.   Almost always the leader, the first servant of the state—has been
confused with the representative of the genius of humanity, who belongs
to the whole of *society* or the people. Among the people, as has already
been observed, everything is *spectacle*—it follows that the spirit of the
people must also be visible. This visible spirit will come either, as in the
millennium, without our help—or it will be chosen unanimously by
open or tacit agreement.

There are many interesting moments in history which are relevant
here—for example, in some places in India the general and the priest
were separate, and the general took second place.

The priest must not lead us astray. In the beginning poet and priest were
one—and only later ages have separated them. But the true poet has
always remained a priest, just as the true priest has always remained a
poet—and ought not the future bring the old state of affairs back again?
That representative of the genius of humanity could easily be the poet *kat
exochen.*[18]

But besides, it is an incontrovertible fact that most princes were not actually princes—but usually more or less a kind of *representative of the genius*

of their age, and the government found itself for the most part, as was fitting, in the hands of subordinates.

76.   Our everyday life consists of nothing but life-sustaining tasks which recur again and again. This cycle of habits is only the means to a principal means, that of our whole earthly being—which is a mixture of diverse ways of existing.

Philistines live only an everyday life. The principal means seems their only purpose. They do all that for the sake of earthly life, it seems, and it must seem so according to their own utterances. They mix poetry with it only in case of *necessity*, simply because they are used to a certain interruption of their daily habits. As a rule this interruption occurs every seven days—and could be called a poetic seven-day fever. On Sundays there is a day of rest—they live a little better than usual and this Sunday indulgence ends with a somewhat deeper sleep than otherwise; therefore on Mondays too everything still moves at a somewhat faster pace. Their *parties de plaisir* must be conventional, ordinary, modish—but as with everything, they deal with their pleasure laboriously and formally. They reach the highest level of their poetic existence in a journey, a wedding, the baptism of a child, and in the church. Here their boldest wishes are satisfied, and often exceeded.

Their so-called religion merely works as an opiate—stimulating—numbing—alleviating pains by weakening. Their morning and evening prayers are as necessary to them as breakfast and supper. They cannot do without them any more. The coarse Philistine imagines the pleasures of heaven in the guise of a church festival—a wedding—a journey or a ball. The refined one—makes of heaven a splendid church—with beautiful music, much pomp—with seats for the common people in the parterre, and chapels and balconies for the more distinguished.

The worst among them are the revolutionary Philistines, who also include the dregs of progressive minds, the race of the covetous.

Gross self-interest is the necessary result of wretched narrowmindedness. To a poor creature, his present sensation is the most lively, the highest attainable. He knows nothing higher than this. No wonder that his understanding, perforce trained by external circumstances—is only the cunning slave of such a dull master and thinks and cares only for his base pleasures.

77.   In the earliest times of the discovery of the faculty of judgment, every new judgment was a find. The worth of this find rose, the more

practicable and fertile the judgment was. Verdicts which now seem to us very common then still demanded an unusual level of intellectual life. One had to bring genius and acuity together in order to find new relations using the new tool. Its application to the most characteristic, interesting, and general aspects of humanity necessarily aroused exceptional admiration and drew the attention of all good minds to itself. In this way those bodies of proverbial sayings came into being that have been valued so highly at all times and among all peoples. It would easily be possible for the discoveries of genius we make today to meet with a similar fate in the course of time. There could easily come a time when all that would be as common as moral precepts are now, and new, more sublime discoveries would occupy the restless spirit of men.

78.   A law is of its nature effective. An ineffective law is no law. Law is a causal concept—a mixture of power and thought. Hence one is never conscious of a law as such. In so far as one thinks of a law it is only a proposition, that is, a thought connected to a capacity—a resisting, tenacious thought is an active thought and links the law and the simple thought.

79.   Excessive readiness to function on the part of the bodily organs would be dangerous for earthly existence. In its present condition the mind would make destructive use of them. A certain *heaviness* of the organ hinders the mind from freely acting at will, and tempts it to cooperate in a regular fashion, as is proper for the earthly world. It is because of the imperfect condition of the mind that this cooperation so exclusively binds it to this world—therefore the cooperation, according to its own principle, is temporary.

80.   Legal theory corresponds to physiology—morals to psychology. The rational principles of the theory of law and morals, transformed into laws of nature, provide the foundations of physiology and psychology.

81.   Flight from the common spirit is death.

82.   In most religious systems we are regarded as parts of the godhead which, if they do not obey the impulses of the whole, and even if they do not intentionally act against the laws of the whole, but only go their own way and do not want to be parts of it, are medically treated by the godhead—and either endure a painful cure or even are cut off.

83.   Every specific stimulus betrays a specific meaning. The newer it is the coarser but also the stronger it is—the more precise, the more pol-

ished and diverse it becomes, the weaker it is. Thus the first thought of God aroused a violent emotion in the whole individual—so too the first idea of philosophy—of humanity, the universe etc.

84.   *The most intimate community of all knowledge*—the republic of learning is the high purpose of scholars.

85.   Ought not the distance of a particular branch of learning from the common level—and thus the standing of the different branches among themselves—to be calculated according to the number of their basic principles? The fewer principles, the higher the learning.

86.   We usually understand the artificial better than the natural. More spirit is needed for the simple than the complicated—but less talent.

87.   Tools arm the human being. One can indeed say that a human being understands how to bring forth a world—he lacks only a suitable contrivance—the appropriate armature of his sense tools. The beginning is there. Thus the principle of a warship lies in the idea of the ship builder, who is able to give body to this thought with the help of large numbers of people and suitable tools and materials—making himself by all this into an enormous machine, as it were.
Thus the idea of a moment would often demand enormous implements—enormous masses of material, and the human being is thus, if not *actu*, then *potentia*, a creator.

88.   In every contact a substance is created the effect of which lasts as long as the contact. This is how all synthetic modifications of the individual come about.
But there are one-sided and mutual contacts—the former are the foundation for the latter.

89.   The more ignorant one is by nature, the more capacity one has for knowledge. Each new insight makes a much deeper, livelier impression. One notices this clearly when embarking on a new branch of learning. That is why one loses capacity through too much studying. It is a kind of ignorance that is opposed to one's initial ignorance. The first kind is ignorance from lack of knowledge—the second from excess of knowledge. The latter customarily has the symptoms of skepticism—but it is a spurious skepticism—deriving from indirect weakness in our capacity for knowledge. One is not in a position to permeate the mass and bring it perfectly to life in a certain form—the *power to give plastic form* is not suffi-

cient. Thus the spirit of invention of young minds, and of enthusiasts—as well as the happy touch of the inspired beginner or the layperson is easily explained.

90.   Building worlds is not enough for the mind that reaches more deeply,
Yet a loving heart is ample for the spirit that constantly strives.[19]

91.   We are related to all parts of the universe—as we are to the future and to times past.
Which relation we establish as the primary one, which one is primarily important—and which is to become effective for us—depends only on the direction and persistence of our attention. It is probable that a truly scientific method for this process is nothing less than the art of invention we have desired for so long—it might indeed be even more than this. The human being acts every hour according to the laws of this art, and it is undoubtedly possible to find these through highly creative self-observation.

92.   The historian endows historical beings with living form. The data of history are the mass which the historian shapes—giving it life. It follows that history also obeys all the principles of animation and of all living form, and until these principles are in place there are also no real products of the historian's art—but only traces here and there of chance animations, where *involuntary* genius was active.

93.   Almost all genius up to now was one-sided—the result of a sickly constitution. One type had too much sense of the external, the other too much inner sense. Seldom could nature achieve a balance between the two—a complete constitution of genius. Often a perfect proportion arose by chance, but this could never endure because it was not comprehended and fixed by the spirit—they remained fortunate moments. The first genius *that penetrated itself* found here the exemplary germ of an immeasurable world. It made a discovery which must have been the most remarkable in the history of the world—for with it there begins a whole new epoch for humanity—and true history of all kinds becomes possible for the first time at this stage—for the way that had been traversed hitherto now makes up a *proper* whole that can be entirely elucidated. That point outside the world is given, and now Archimedes can fulfil his promise.[20]

94.   Before abstraction everything is one—but it is one as chaos is—after abstraction everything is again unified—but this unification is a free

alliance of independent, self-determined beings. A crowd has become a society — chaos is transformed into a manifold world.[21]

95.　If the world is as it were a precipitate of human nature, then the world of the gods is a sublimate of it. Both occur *uno actu*. No precipitation without sublimation. The agility lost there is gained here.

96.　Where children are, there is a golden age.

97.　Security for themselves and for the invisible powers was the basis of the clerical states up to now.

98.　The process of approximation is made up of increasing steps forward and backward. Both delay it — both hasten it — both lead to the goal. Thus in the novel the writer seems now to approach the goal, now to retreat again, and it is never closer than when it seems to be most distant.

99.　A criminal cannot complain about injustice if he is treated harshly and inhumanely. His crime meant entering into the realm of violence, of tyranny. In this world there is no moderation or proportion — hence he must not be astonished in the face of excessive countermeasures.

100. The wisdom of story telling contains the history of the archetypal world — it embraces times past, present, and future.
The human world is the common instrument of the gods. Poetry unites them as it does us.

101. That which the external world perceives as quite motionless has the appearance of being quite *at rest*. However much it may change, in relation to the external world it always stays at rest. This principle governs all self-modifications. That is why the beautiful appears so much at rest. Everything beautiful is a *self-illuminated*, perfect individual.

102. Every human form brings to life an individual germ in the beholder. This gaze becomes infinite thereby — it is bound up with a feeling of inexhaustible power — and therefore it vivifies so absolutely. As we behold ourselves — we give ourselves life.
Without this visible and tangible immortality — *sit venia verbis* — we would not truly be able to think.
This perceptible inadequacy of the earthly bodily form as the expression and instrument of the spirit dwelling within is the undefined, driving thought which becomes the basis of all true thoughts — the cause of the evolution of intelligence — that which obliges us to assume an intelligible

world and an infinite series of expressions and instruments of each spirit, whose index or root is its individuality.

103. The more narrow-minded a system is the more it will please worldly-wise people. Thus the system of the materialists, the doctrine of Helvetius and also Locke has received the most acclaim amongst this class. Thus Kant even now will find more followers than Fichte.

104. The art of writing books has not yet been invented. But it is on the point of being invented. Fragments of this kind are literary seedings. Many among them may indeed be sterile — still if only some grow.[22]

105. Schlegel's writings are lyrical philosophemes. His essays on Forster and Lessing are outstanding examples of minus poetry and resemble the Pindaric hymns.[23] The lyrical prose writer will write logical epigrams. If he is quite intoxicated with life they will be dithyrambs, which one must of course enjoy and judge as dithyrambs. A work of art can be half-intoxicated — but in a state of complete intoxication the work of art will dissolve. The human being becomes an animal — the character of the animal is dithyrambic. The animal is an oversaturated form of life — the plant is a deficient form of life. The human being is a *free* form of life.

106. Hemsterhuis is very often a follower of Homer in logic.

107. Goethe's philosophemes are truly epic.

108. If the spirit sanctifies it, then every true book is a bible.

109. Every individual is the center of a system of emanation.[24]

110. If spirit resembles precious metal then most books are the cheapest coins.
Every *useful* book must at least have a large amount of alloy. In its pure state precious metal cannot be used for everyday business matters.
It is so rare that a book is written for the sake of the book.
It happens with many genuine books as it does with lumps of gold in Ireland. They serve many years only as weights.
Our books are an informal kind of paper money that scholars put into circulation. The popularity of paper money in the modern world is the soil on which they sprout and grow, often in one night.

111. Many books are longer than they seem. They have indeed no end. The boredom that they cause is truly absolute and infinite. Model exam-

ples of this kind have been provided by Professors Heydenreich, Jakob, Abicht, and Pölitz.[25] Here is a stock to which anyone can add with his acquaintances of the kind.

112. In very many writings the argument of the author, or that mass to which the facts and experiences are attached, is a convergence of the most remarkable psychic phenomena—extremely informative for the anthropognostic[26]—full of traces of asthenic dispositions and indirect inflammations.[27]

113. Reviewers are literary policemen. Doctors are policemen also. Hence there ought to be critical journals which treat authors with medical and surgical methods, and not merely find out the ailment and announce it with malicious pleasure. Methods of healing up to now have been barbaric for the most part.
A genuine police force is not merely defensive and polemical toward whatever evil exists—but it seeks to improve the sickly disposition.

114. The *Allgemeine Litteratur Zeitung* is like those people who, out of attachment to the good things of this life, seek only to maintain life as long as possible.[28] Hufeland's macrobiotics was put into practice even earlier by the dispatchers of the *Allgemeine Litteratur Zeitung*.[29] In the beginning the paper was debauched by new ideas. It had a weak constitution all along. Long use of Kantian concepts did it much damage. Now it has become more vigilant and is trying to prolong the golden dream of earthly existence for itself as long as possible by a diet of fasting, only occasional use of spirituous liquors, and accommodation to the influence of the weather, according to Hufeland's highly praised principle of moderation.

115. Many antirevolutionary books have been written for the Revolution. But Burke has written a revolutionary book against the Revolution.[30]

116. Most observers of the Revolution, especially the clever and distinguished ones, have declared it to be a life-threatening and contagious illness—they stuck fast at the symptoms, mixed them up and explained them in various ways—many regarded it as merely a local illness—the most brilliant opponents urged castration. They did indeed notice—that this supposed illness was nothing but a crisis of incipient puberty.

117. Is it not eminently desirable—to be the contemporary of a truly great man? The majority of cultivated Germans today is not of this opin-

ion—they are grand enough to deny all greatness and they follow a course of leveling. If the Copernican system were not so firmly entrenched it would be very easy for them—to make the sun and the stars into will-o'-the-wisps again and the earth into the universe. Hence a great man among us now is treated as meanly as possible—and regarded with disdain if he does not answer to what is customarily expected for entertainment, and causes these people a moment's discomfort with themselves. An interesting symptom of this direct weakness of mind is the reception of *Hermann und Dorothea*.[31]

118. Goethe is now the true representative of the poetic spirit on earth.

119. To describe people has been impossible up to now because what a person is was not known. As soon as what a person is becomes known it will also be possible to describe the true genesis of individuals.

120. He who wants to hold fragments of this kind to their promise may be an honorable man—only he is not to pretend to be a poet. Must one always be deliberate? He who is too old for enthusiasm should avoid meeting young people. Now there are literary saturnalia—the more colorful life is the better.

121. The geognostics believe that the physical center of gravity lies under Fez and Morocco—Goethe, as an anthropognostic, maintains in *Meister* that the intellectual center of gravity lies under the German nation.[32]

122. Where the majority decides—energy rules over form. It is the converse where the minority has the upper hand.
One cannot reproach the political theorists with audacity. Has it never occurred to any of them to explore whether monarchy and democracy could and ought to be simply combined, as elements of a true universal state?[33]
A true democracy is an absolute minus-state. A true monarchy is an absolute plus-state. The constitution of the monarchy is the character of the ruler. Its guarantee is his will.
Democracy in the usual sense is not fundamentally different from monarchy, only that then the monarch is a head made up of many minds. True democracy is Protestantism—a political state of nature, as Protestantism in the narrower sense is a religious state of nature.
The moderate form of government is half political entity and half state of nature. It is an artificial, very fragile *machine*—therefore it is highly offen-

sive to all minds of genius—but it is the hobbyhorse of our time. If this machine could be transformed into a living, autonomous being, then the great problem would be solved. The arbitrariness of nature and the constraint of art permeate each other, if they are dissolved in spirit. The spirit makes both of them fluid. The spirit is always poetic. The poetic state is the true, perfect state.

A state imbued with spirit will be poetic of itself. The more spirit and spiritual intercourse there is in the state the more it will approach the poetic state—the more joyfully everyone in it will curb his claims and want to make the necessary sacrifices out of love for the beautiful, great *individuo*—the less will the state stand in need of [making sacrifices]. The spirit of the state will more closely resemble the spirit of a single exemplary person—who has only ever enunciated a sole law to endure forever: be as good and poetic as possible.

123. Nothing is more poetic than memory and premonition, or the conception of the future. The everyday present joins both of these together through limitation. Contiguity comes into being through atrophy—crystallization. But there is a spiritual present—which fuses them together through dissolving them—and this mixture is the element, the atmosphere of the poet. What is not spirit is matter.

124. The conceptions of times past draw us toward dying—toward disintegration. The conceptions of the future—drive us toward living forms—to incorporation, the action of assimilation.

Hence all memory is melancholy—all premonition joyful. The former moderates excessive liveliness—the latter is uplifting for life that is too weak.

125. The true reader must be an extension of the author. He is the higher court that receives the case already prepared by the lower court. The feeling by means of which the author has separated out the materials of his work, during reading separates out again the unformed and the formed aspects of the book—and if the reader were to work through the book according to his own idea, a second reader would refine it still more, with the result that, since the mass that had been worked through would constantly be poured into fresh vessels, the mass would finally become an essential component—a part of the active spirit.

Through *impartial* rereading of his book the author can refine his book himself. With strangers the particular character is usually lost, because the talent of fully entering into another person's idea is so rare. Often even in the author himself. It is not a sign of superior education and greater powers to justifiably find fault with a book. When receiving new impressions, greater sharpness of mind is quite natural.

2 *Logological Fragments I*

1.   The history of philosophy up to now is nothing but a history of attempts to discover how to do philosophy. As soon as we do philosophy — philosophemes come into being, and the true natural history of philosophemes is *philosophy*.[1]

2.   These diverse views from the years of my philosophical education can perhaps entertain someone who enjoys observing the development of nature, and may not be a waste of time for one who is himself still engaged in studying philosophy.

3.   The letter is only an aid to philosophical communication, the actual essence of which consists in arousing a particular train of thought. Someone speaking thinks and produces — someone listening reflects — and reproduces. Words are a deceptive medium for what is already thought — unreliable vehicles of a particular, specific stimulus. The true teacher is a guide. If the pupil genuinely desires truth it requires only a *hint* to show him how to find what he is seeking. Accordingly the representation of philosophy consists purely of themes — of initial propositions — principles. It exists only for autonomous lovers of truth. The analytical exposition of the theme is only for those who are sluggish or unpracticed. The latter must learn thereby how to fly and keep themselves moving in a particular direction.

Attentiveness is a centripetal force. The effective relation between that which is directed and the object of the direction begins with the given direction. If we hold fast to this direction we are apodictically certain of reaching the goal that has been set.

47

True *collaboration in philosophy*[2] then is a common movement toward a beloved world—whereby we relieve each other in the most advanced outpost, a movement that demands the greatest effort against the resisting element within which we are flying.

4.   A problem is a solid, synthetic mass which is broken up by means of the penetrating power of the mind. Thus, conversely, fire is nature's mental power and each *body* is a *problem*.

5.   In all philosophy one must be able to distinguish the contingent from the essential. This contingent aspect includes its polemical side. In later ages the effort wasted on the refutation and repudiation of earlier opinions appears strange indeed. This polemic is actually a campaign against oneself—while the thinker who has outgrown his own time is still discomforted by the prejudices of his student years—a discomfort that we can no longer conceive of in more enlightened times, because we feel no need to secure ourselves against it.

6.   Every word is a word to conjure with. Whichever spirit calls— another such appears.

7.   When one begins to reflect on philosophy—then philosophy seems to us to be everything, like God, and love. It is a mystical, highly potent, *penetrating* idea—which ceaselessly drives us inward in all directions. The decision to do philosophy—to seek philosophy is the act of self-liberation—the thrust toward ourselves.

8.   As well as the philosophy of philosophy there are other philosophies, it is true—which one might call individual philosophies. The method is genuinely philosophical. They start from the absolute—but not from a pure absolute. Hence they are really a mixture of philosophy and nonphilosophy, and the more dense the mixture the more interesting they are. They are entirely individual—they forcefully posit a synthesis as a thesis. The representation of the philosophy of philosophy will always have something of an individual philosophy in it. Equally the poet represents only individual philosophy, and moreover anyone, no matter how vigorously he may acknowledge the philosophy of philosophy, will in practical terms be only more or less an individual philosopher, and despite all his striving he will never be entirely able to step out of the magic circle of his individual philosophy.

9. Should the highest principle include the highest paradox in its function? To be a proposition that would allow absolutely no peace—which
would always attract and repel—always become impenetrable again, no
matter how often one had already understood it? Which would ceaselessly arouse our activity—without ever tiring it or becoming familiar?
According to old mystical legends God is something like that for the spirits.

10. Up to now our thinking was either purely mechanical—*discursive*—
atomistic—or purely intuitive—dynamic. Perhaps now the time for union
has come?

11. It might well be possible that Fichte is the inventor of an entirely
new way of thinking—for which language has as yet no name. The inventor is perhaps not the most perfect and ingenious artist on his instrument—although I am not saying that this is the case. But it is probable
that people exist and will exist—who are far better able to Fichtecize than
Fichte himself.[3] *Wonderful works of art* could come into being in this
way—as soon as we have learnt to Fichtecize artistically.

12. In the truest sense doing philosophy is—a caress. It bears witness to
the deepest love of reflection, to absolute delight in wisdom.

13. The crude, discursive thinker is the scholastic. The true scholastic is
given to mystical subtleties. He builds his universe out of logical atoms.
He destroys all living nature in order to put a mental trick in its place—his
goal is an infinite automaton. His opposite is the crude, intuitive poet. He
is given to mystical macrology.[4] He hates rules and fixed form. Wild, violent life reigns in nature—everything is vivified. There is no law—but
only the arbitrary and the miraculous everywhere. He is purely dynamic.
Thus the philosophical spirit stirs at first in completely separate masses.
At the second stage of civilization these masses begin to touch each
other—in sufficiently diverse ways. Just as it is only the union of infinite
extremes that gives rise at all to the finite, the limited, so here too countless eclectics now emerge. The age of misunderstandings begins. At this
stage the most limited thinker is the most important, he is the purest
philosopher of the second stage. This class is entirely confined to the real,
the present world, in the strictest sense. The philosophers of the first class
look down with disdain on this second one. They say, all those people
amount to very little—and consequently nothing at all. The first class
regards the views of the second as stemming from weakness, as inconse-

quence. Conversely, the second class agrees in pitying the first—whom they hold guilty of the most absurd mystification to the point of delusion. If from one point of view the scholastics and the alchemists seem to be completely at variance with one another, but the eclectics on the contrary to be at one, from the reverse angle everything is exactly the other way round. Essentially the former are indirectly of one mind—namely on the absolute independence and tendency toward the infinite of meditation. Both start from the absolute—on the other hand the narrow-minded ones are essentially at odds with each other and can only agree in derivative matters. The former are infinite, but uniform—the latter limited—but diverse. The former have genius—the latter talent—the former ideas—the latter skills. The former are heads, without hands, the latter hands, without heads.

The ascent to the third stage is achieved by the artist, who is at once tool and genius. He finds that this original division of absolute philosophical activities is a deeper division of his own being—whose survival rests on the possibility of its mediation—its combination. He finds that, no matter how heterogeneous these activities are, there is nonetheless a capacity within himself to move from one to the other, to change his polarity at will. Thus he discovers in them the necessary elements of his spirit—he perceives that both must be united in a common principle. He concludes from this that eclecticism is nothing but the result of the incomplete, deficient use of this capacity. It appears to him more than probable that the reason for this incompleteness lies in the weakness of the productive imagination—which at the moment of transition from one element to the other could not remain suspended in contemplation of itself. The complete representation of true spiritual life, raised to consciousness through this action, is *philosophy kat exochen*. Here that *living* reflection comes into being, which with careful tending afterwards extends of itself into an infinitely formed spiritual universe—the kernel or germ of an all-encompassing organism. It is the beginning of a true *self-penetration of the spirit* which never ends.

14.   Sophists are people who, alert to the weaknesses and errors of philosophers, seek to use these to their advantage or generally for certain unphilosophical, unworthy purposes—often philosophy itself. Thus they actually have nothing to do with philosophy. If they are unphilosophical on principle—then they are to be regarded as enemies of philosophy and to be treated as enemies. The most dangerous class among them are those

who are skeptics *out of pure hatred of philosophy*. The other skeptics are in part very worthy of respect. They are the forerunners of the third period. They have the genuine philosophical gift of discrimination — and they lack only spiritual potency. They have the required capacity — but not the self-motivating force. They feel the inadequacy of earlier systems — none *vivifies* them entirely. They have genuine taste — but the necessary energy of the productive imagination is lacking. They must be polemical. All eclectics are really skeptics. The more they embrace, the more skeptical they are — this last observation is confirmed by the fact that the greatest and best scholars hitherto acknowledged at the end of their lives that they *knew* the least.

15.   Common logic is the grammar of higher language or thought. It comprises merely the relations of concepts with each other — the mechanics of thinking — the pure physiology of concepts. But logical concepts relate to each other as words do, without thoughts.

Logic is concerned simply with the dead body of the philosophy of mind. Metaphysics is the pure dynamics of thinking. It is about original mental powers — it is concerned simply with the soul of the philosophy of mind. Metaphysical concepts relate to each other like *thoughts, without words*. People have often wondered at the persistent incompleteness of both branches of philosophy. Each of them went ahead in its own way, and there are flaws everywhere. Neither was ever quite in order. Right from the beginning people sought to unite them, since every aspect of them pointed to an affinity. But every attempt failed — since one of the two always suffered as a result and lost its essential character. What was left was metaphysical logic — and logical metaphysics — but neither was what it should have been. It was no better with physiology and psychology or mechanics and chemistry. In the last half of this century a new inflammation arose here that was more violent than ever — hostile masses towered up against each other more strongly than ever before — the ferment was unbounded — mighty explosions resulted. Some people maintain now that somewhere true penetration has occurred — a germ of union has come into being that would gradually grow and assimilate everything in one indivisible form. They believe that this principle of eternal peace is moving irresistibly in all directions, and soon there will be only one philosophy and one spirit, one prophet and one god.

16.   The perfect form of the different branches of learning must be poetic. Every proposition must have independent character—must be a self-evident whole, the seedpod of a witty idea.

17.   The first synthetic proposition is like the first kernel. It detaches itself from the two premises one proposition after the next, according to the laws of attraction of the kernel, and by means of its passage through the first proposition it is assimilated to the second—and so philosophy grows toward infinity, outward and inward. It strives as it were to fill the infinite space between the premises.[5]

18.   The greatest problems occupy humanity earliest. On first reflection the human being feels extremely forcibly the need to unite the highest ends. As civilization advances his attempts begin to lose the quality of genius—but they gain in utility—whereby he is led into the error—of generalizing entirely from the premises, and of pursuing the ambition merely to unite closer conditional terms. But it is inevitable that he soon notices the necessary deficiency of this method and looks for a possible way of combining the advantages of the first method with the advantages of the second, thereby completing both. Now it occurs to him at last to seek within himself, as the absolute center of these divided worlds, the absolute copula. He sees suddenly that in reality the problem is already solved by his existence—and that consciousness of the laws of his existence is knowledge *kat exochen*, which he has been seeking for so long. Through the discovery of this consciousness the great puzzle is largely solved. Just as his life is real philosophy, so his philosophy is ideal life—the living theory of life. Chance facts become systematic experiments. His path is now laid out for him for all eternity. He is concerned with the extension of his existence into infinity—the dream of his youth has become a beautiful reality—his earlier hopes and expectations have become symbolic prophecies. The apparent contradiction in the original problem—of the problems—solution and nonsolution at once—is completely resolved.

19.   Instead of cosmogonies and theogonies our philosophers busy themselves with anthropogonies.

20.   There are certain poetic works within us that have quite a different character from the others, for they are accompanied by a sense of necessity, and yet there exists simply no other external reason for them. A person believes he is involved in a conversation, and some kind of unknown,

spiritual being in a miraculous way causes him to think the most obvious thoughts. This being must be a higher being, because it communicates with him in a way that is not possible for any being which is bound to appearances. It must be a like being, because it treats him like a spiritual being and only requires the rarest independent activity of him. This higher kind of self has the same relation to the human being as the human being has to nature or the wise man to the child. The human being yearns to be the equal of this being in the same way as he seeks to make himself the equal of the nonself.

This fact cannot be demonstrated. Everyone must experience it for himself. It is a fact of a higher kind that will be encountered only by the higher man. But people should strive to bring it about in themselves.

The kind of knowledge that arises in this way is the higher theory of knowledge.[6] Here the proposition: self determines nonself—is the principle of the theoretical part, and the proposition: self is determined—is the principle of the practical part. The practical part comprises the self-education of the self toward becoming capable of that communication [with a higher being]—the theoretical part comprises the characteristics of genuine communication. Rites are part of education.

In Fichte the theoretical part comprises the characteristics of a true idea—the practical part comprises the education and formation of the nonself toward becoming capable of experiencing a true influence, a true communion with the self—thereby also the parallel self-formation of the self.

Morality thus belongs in both worlds; here, as an end—there as a means—and it is the bond that binds them both together.

21. Doing philosophy is a conversation with oneself of the above kind—an actual revelation of the self—arousal of the real self through the ideal self. Doing philosophy is the foundation of all other revelations. The decision to do philosophy is a challenge to the real self to reflect, to awaken and to be spirit. Without philosophy there is no true morality, and without morality no philosophy.

22. The possibility of all philosophy rests on the fact—that the intelligence endows itself with self-regulated movement—that is, its own form of activity—through acting on itself.

23. If the world is like a precipitate of human nature, then the world of the gods is a sublimate—both occur *uno actu*. No material precipitate without a spiritual sublimate. What the former loses in heat the latter

gains. God and world come into being at once in a single transformation—through a dissolution of human nature. Good and bad spirits are like air and nitrogen. For animal life both are necessary—and the animal body consists for the most part of bad spiritual matter.

24.   The poem of the understanding is philosophy. It is the greatest impetus that the understanding gives itself about itself—union of the *understanding* and the *imagination*. Without philosophy a person remains divided in his most essential powers. He is two people—one who has understanding—and one who is a poet.

Without philosophy a poet is incomplete. Without philosophy a thinker—or a judge—is incomplete.

25.   Poetry elevates each single thing through a particular combination with the rest of the whole—and if it is philosophy that first prepares the world through its legislation for the active influence of ideas, then poetry is at it were the key to philosophy, its purpose and meaning; for poetry shapes the beautiful society—the world family—the beautiful household of the universe.[7]

Just as philosophy *strengthens* the *powers* of the individual with the powers of humanity and the universe through system and the state, making the whole the instrument of the individual and the individual the instrument of the whole—in the same way poetry functions in respect of *life*. The individual lives in the whole and the whole in the individual. Through poetry there arises the highest sympathy and common activity, the most intimate *communion* of the finite and the infinite.

26.   The poet ends the move as he begins it. If the philosopher only orders everything, places everything, the poet would loosen all bonds. His words are not common signs—they are sounds—magic words which move beautiful groups around themselves. As the garments of the saints still retain wondrous powers, so is many a word sanctified through some splendid memory, and has become a poem almost on its own. For the poet language is never too poor but always too general. He needs words that often recur and are played out through use. His world is simple, like his instrument—but it is just as inexhaustible a source of melodies.

27.   Everything that surrounds us, daily incidents, ordinary circumstances, the habits of our way of life, exercises an uninterrupted influence on us, which for just that reason is imperceptible but extremely important. However beneficial and useful this circulation is for us, in so far as

we are contemporaries at a certain time or members of a specific body, we are nevertheless hindered by it in the higher development of our nature. Divinatory, magical, truly poetic people cannot come into being under circumstances such as ours.

28.   For savages a poem is a story without a beginning, a middle, and an end—the pleasure they experience in it is merely emotional—a simple pastime, merely the dynamic quickening of the imagination.
The epic poem is a noble version of the primitive poem. In essence it is exactly the same.
The novel is far above that. The former lives on—the latter grows as it lives—in the former there is arithmetical, in the novel geometrical progression.[8]

29.   He who cannot make poems will also be only able to judge them negatively. True criticism requires the ability to create the product to be criticized oneself. Taste alone only judges negatively.

30.   Writing poetry is creating. Each work of literature must be a living individual. What an inexhaustible amount of materials for *new* individual combinations is lying about! Anyone who has once guessed this secret—needs nothing more than to decide to renounce endless variety and the mere enjoyment of it and to *start* somewhere—but this decision is at the expense of the free feeling of an infinite world—and demands restriction to a single appearance of it.
Ought we perhaps to attribute our earthly existence to a similar decision?

31.   Poetry is the basis of society as virtue is the basis of the state. Religion is a mixture of poetry and virtue—can you guess, then—what it is the basis of?

32.   The artist stands on the human being as a statue does on a pedestal.

33.   As the mass is connected to the beautiful outline, so is the passionate with description in the work of art.

34.   The artist is completely transcendental.

35.   The actor vivifies in himself the principle of a particular individuality *by choice*.
There is a symptomatic and a genetic form of imitation. Only the last is alive. It presupposes the closest union of imagination and understanding.

This capacity to truly awaken an individuality not one's own within one-self—not merely to deceive through superficial imitation—is still entirely unknown—and rests on a most marvelous power of *penetration* and spiritual acting. The artist turns himself into everything he sees and wants to be.

36.   Poetry is the great art of the construction of transcendental health. The poet is thus the transcendental physician.
Poetry holds sway with pain and titillation—with pleasure and discomfort—error and truth—health and illness. It mixes everything together for the sake of its great purpose of all purposes—the *elevation of the human being above himself.*

37.   As earlier philosophies are to logology, so earlier forms of poetry are to the poetry that is to come.
Earlier forms of poetry were mostly effective dynamically, the transcendental poetry of the future could be called organic. When it is invented it will be seen that all true poets up to now made poetry organically *without knowing it*—but that this lack of consciousness of what they were doing— had a substantial influence on the whole of their work—so that for the most part they were only poetic in details—but the whole was usually unpoetic. Logology will necessarily bring about this revolution.

38.   The content of the drama is a becoming or a passing away. It comprises the representation of the origin of an organic form from what was fluid—a well-ordered event from chance. It comprises the representation of the dissolution—the passing away of an organic form as chance. It can contain both at once and then it is a complete drama. It can easily be seen that the content of such a work must be a transformation—a process of purification or reduction. *Oedipus at Colonos* is a fine example of it—so also is *Philoctetes.*

39.   Goethe's *Fairy-Tale* is opera told as a story.[9]

40.   Poetry dissolves the being of others in its own.

41.   Transcendental poetry is a mixture of philosophy and poetry. It really embraces all transcendental functions, indeed it comprises the transcendental altogether. The transcendental poet is the transcendental person altogether.

42.   From the study of transcendental poetry a tropology can be antici-
pated—which comprehends the laws of the *symbolic construction* of the
transcendental world.

43.   Genius in general is poetic. Where genius has been active it has
been poetically active. The truly moral person is a poet.

44.   The true beginning is nature poetry. The end is the second beginning—and is art poetry.[10]

45.   It is a nice point whether the lyric poem would actually be *poem*,
plus-poetry, or prose, minus-poetry.[11] Just as the novel has been taken for
prose, so the lyric poem has been taken for poetry—both unjustly. The
highest, most authentic prose is the lyric poem.
What is called prose had its origin in the limitation of absolute extremes.
It only exists ad interim and plays a subaltern, temporal role. There will
come a time when it will not exist any more. Then limitation will have
turned into penetration. True life has come into being, and prose and
poetry are thereby most closely united and made interchangeable.

46.   As the epic, lyric and dramatic ages succeeded one another in the
history of Greek poetry, so in the universal history of poetry the ancient,
modern, and unified periods succeed one another. The interesting is the
subject of minus-poetry.[12]
In Goethe a seed of this union seems to have begun to shoot. Anyone who
guesses how this happened has created the possibility of a perfect history
of poetry.

47.   In the ancient world religion already was to a certain extent what it
will become for us—practical poetry.

48.   Voltaire is one of the greatest minus-poets who ever lived. His
Candide is his *Odyssey*. It is a pity for him that his world was a Parisian
boudoir. With less personal and national vanity he would have been
much more.

49.   All representation of the past is tragedy in the true sense. All representation of what is to come—of the future—is comedy. Tragedy takes its
rightful place in the richest life of a people—as comedy belongs in its
poor life. In England and France tragedies would now be very appropriate, whereas in Germany there should be comedies.

50.   One should never see painting or sculpture without music—
whereas music should be heard in beautifully decorated rooms.
But poetry should never be enjoyed without the plastic arts and music at
the same time. That is why poetry is so extraordinarily effective in a beautiful theater or in churches decorated with taste. In all good society music
should be heard at intervals. It was because it was felt that the decorative
arts were necessary for true sociability that reception rooms were devised.
Better food, social games, more elegant clothes, dancing, and even more
polished, freer, more general conversation arose through this sense of
higher life in society and the resulting mixture of everything beautiful and
vivifying in many different kinds of overall effects.

51.   *The lyric poem is the chorus in the drama of life—of the world.
Lyric poets are a chorus sweetly mixed of youth and age, joy, sympathy
and wisdom.

52.   On interesting regents—who fruitfully *extended the art of government* with new ideas, and gave their contemporaries and their reign great
individual character—to whom humanity owes progress and enlightenment on a large scale. In this century perhaps only Peter the Great and
Joseph II. Frederick the Great at least does not quite belong under this
rubric. There were more interesting people among the regents.

53.   *Mystical faith and dependence on that which now exists, the old
and well-known—and mystical hope and joy in everything to come—the
new, unknown—these are two very important character traits of humanity hitherto.

54.   *Just as nothing is free, so also nothing can be compelled but the
spirit. Only a spirit can be compelled to something. Therefore that which
may be compelled is spirit, insofar as it may be compelled.

55.   *We seek the *design* for the world—we are this design ourselves.
What are we? Personified *all-powerful points*. But the execution, as the
image of the design, must also be equal to it in free activity and self-refer-
ence—and vice versa. Thus the life or being of the spirit consists in conceiving, bearing and educating its own kind. Only in so far then as the
human being lives a happily married life with himself—and comprises a
beautiful family, is he capable of marriage and family at all. Act of
embracing oneself.
One must never confess to oneself that one loves oneself. The secret of
this confession is the life principle of the one true and eternal love. The

first kiss in this understanding is the principle of philosophy—the origin of a new world—the beginning of absolute chronology—the completion of an infinitely growing bond with the self.

Who would not like a philosophy whose germ is a first kiss?

Love popularises the personality—it makes individual things *communicable* and *understandable*. (Understanding of love).

56.   What more can we want if we have good, upright parents, friends deserving of respect and affection, gifted and diverse acquaintances, a blameless reputation, a comely figure, a way of life comme il faut, a generally healthy body, appropriate occupations, pleasing and useful skills, a serene soul, a moderate income, diverse beauties of nature and art around us, a conscience largely at ease—and either love, the world, and family life still before us—or love beside us, the world behind us, and a successful family around us. I should have thought in the former case nothing but a diligent temperament and patient trust—in the latter case nothing but faith and a kindly death.

57.   *I should wish that my readers were reading the observation that the beginning of philosophy is a first kiss at the moment when they were listening to Mozart's "Wenn die Liebe in Deinen blauen Augen" being performed with true feeling[13]—if they could indeed sense that they were about to experience a first kiss.

On musical accompaniment to different kinds of meditation, conversation, and reading.

58.   If theory were to wait for experience it would never come about.

59.   Self equals nonself—the highest principle of all *learning* and *art*.[14]

60.   On the negative principle of the state—security—and the positive principle of the state—expansion or security in the higher sense. Both affect the other.

Police—and *politics*.

61.   Is there a fine art of *mathematics*? Mystical mathematics. Musical mathematics. Has mathematics merely a finite purpose? Is it not purely theoretical? Truly pure mathematics? Quantities are construed by quantities.

62.   *Difference between *writing poetry* and making a poem. The *understanding* is the epitome of the talents. The reason posits, the imagination

designs — the understanding executes. It is the converse where the imagination *executes* — and the understanding designs.
Romantic and rhetorical poetry.

63.   The eye is the speech-organ of feeling. Visible objects are the expressions of the feelings.

64.   *The meaning of Socratism is that philosophy is *everywhere* or nowhere — and that with little effort one could get one's bearings through the first available means and find what one is seeking. Socratism is the art — of finding out the standpoint of truth from any given vantage point, thus exactly defining the relations of the given to truth.

65.   Formerly all things were spirit appearances. Now we can see nothing but dead repetition, which we do not understand. The meaning of the hieroglyph is missing. We are still living on the fruit of better times.

66.   The world must be made Romantic. In that way one can find the original meaning again. To make Romantic is nothing but a qualitative raising to a higher power.[15] In this operation the lower self will become one with a better self. Just as we ourselves are such a qualitative exponential series. This operation is as yet quite unknown. By endowing the commonplace with a higher meaning, the ordinary with mysterious respect, the known with the dignity of the unknown, the finite with the appearance of the infinite, I am making it Romantic. The operation for the higher, unknown, mystical, infinite is the converse — this undergoes a logarithmic change through this connection — it takes on an ordinary form of expression. Romantic philosophy. *Lingua romana.*[16] Raising and lowering by turns.

67.   It is the same with love as with conviction — how many believe they are convinced, and are not. One can be truly convinced only of the *true* — one can truly love only that which is dear.

68.   All cognition, knowledge etc. may well be reduced to comparisons, resemblances. *everyth re margmal, relative, & reducible*

69.   All true enthusiasts and mystics have without doubt been possessed of higher powers — strange mixtures and shapes have certainly resulted from this. The coarser and more colorful the material, the more lacking in taste, education, and direction the person was, the more eccentric was what he brought forth. It might well be wasted effort for the most part — to clean, refine, and clarify this grotesque (strange) mass — at least the time

has not yet come when such tasks can be performed with little effort. This remains to be achieved by future historians of *magic*. As very important documents of the gradual evolution of magic power they are worthy of careful preservation and collection.

Magic is the art of using the world of the senses at will.

70.   We have two sense systems which, however different they appear, are yet entwined extremely closely with one another. One system is called the body, one the soul. The former is dependent on external stimuli, whose essence we call nature or the external world. The latter originally is dependent on the essence of inner stimuli that we call spirit, or the world of spirits. Usually this last system stands in a nexus of association with the other system—and is affected by it. Nevertheless frequent traces of a converse relation are to be found, and one soon notices that both systems ought actually to stand in a perfect reciprocal relation to one another, in which, while each of them is affected by its world, they should create harmony, not a monotone. In short, both worlds, like both systems, are to create free harmony, not disharmony or monotony. The transition from monotony to harmony certainly will pass through disharmony—and only in the end will harmony ensue. In the age of magic the body serves the soul, or the world of spirits. *Madness—enthusiasm.*

Communal madness ceases to be madness and becomes magic. Madness governed by rules and in full consciousness.

All arts and sciences rest on *partial harmonies.*

Poets, madmen, saints, prophets.

71.   We shall understand the world when we understand ourselves, because we and it are integral *halves.* We are God's children, divine seeds. One day we shall be what our Father is.

72.   On *nonsensory* or *immediate* knowledge. All meaning is *representative—symbolic*—a medium. All sense perception is at secondhand. The more particular, the more abstract, one could say, the idea, the description, or the imitation, the less it resembles the object or the stimulus, the more separate and independent is the meaning. If the meaning did not need an external cause at all it would cease to be meaning and would be a congruous being. As such its forms can again be more or less similar and corresponding to the forms of other beings. Were its forms and their sequence to perfectly resemble the sequence of forms of another being— then there would be the purest harmony between them.

Meaning is a tool—a means. Absolute meaning would be means and end at the same time. Thus every thing is *itself the means* whereby we can come to know it—to experience it or have an effect on it. Thus in order to feel and come to know a thing completely I would have to make it my meaning and object at once—I would have to *vivify it*—make it into absolute meaning, according to the earlier definition.

If however I were neither *able* nor *willing* to do this completely, then I would have to make a part of it—specifically an individual part quite peculiar to the thing—an element of the meaning. What would now ensue? I would acquire mediated and immediate knowledge and experience of the thing at the same time—it would be representative and not representative, perfect and imperfect—my own and not my own, in short it would be both antithetical and synthetic knowledge and experience of it. The element or meaning would be at once an element and a nonelement, because through vivifying it I would in a sense have severed it from the whole.

If I call the whole thing world, then I would have an integral part of the world in myself, and the rest of it outside myself. I would appear to myself in a theoretical respect, with regard to this meaning, as dependent and under the influence of the world.

I would further, *in connection with this meaning*, be obliged to cooperate as an element of the world—for otherwise I would accomplish my intention only incompletely in vivifying it. I would find my meaning, or body, determined partly by itself and partly by the idea of the whole—by its spirit—the world soul, and this so that both are inextricably united—so that properly speaking one could refer neither to the one nor the other exclusively. My body would seem to me not specifically different from the whole—but only a variant of it. My knowledge of the whole would thus have the character of analogy—but this would refer in the closest and most immediate way to the direct and *absolute* knowledge of the element. Both together would comprise an antithetical synthetic knowledge. It would be immediate, and by means of the immediate it would be mediated, at once real and symbolic. All analogy is symbolic. I find my body determined and made effective by itself and the world soul at the same time. My body is a small whole, and thus it also has a special soul; for I call soul the individual principle whereby everything becomes one whole.[17]

I know myself to be as I will and will myself to be as I know—because I *will* my *will*—because I will absolutely. Thus within myself knowledge and will are perfectly united.

While I want to understand my will—and particularly also my deed—I notice that I also have a will and can do something—without knowing about it—further, that I can and do know something *without* having willed it.

73.   Every tool is the vehicle of an utterance or action from outside. It modifies and is modified. The execution is a product of the individual nature of the tool and the use of it. Both can be variable—then the product too will be variable. But a case could arise in which they are able to be changed into their polar opposites—and then the product is *constant* and uniform.

The *shape* (nature) of the *tool* is as it were *one element* of the product. Thus the point is an *element* of the line, the line an element of the plane—the plane an element of the body. This example, it seems to me, illuminates the concept of the element very clearly.

I cannot be effective with a tool in any other way—than in that which its natural relations determine for it. Thus with a chisel I can only strike, scrape, cut, or break, and only if it is made of sharp *iron* use it electrically, or as metal for a galvanic excitator. In both the last cases it is no longer functioning as a chisel. So I feel myself confined by each particular tool to a special kind of activity. I can of course vary this special sphere in an infinite number of ways—I can strike things, break them etc., modify the effect just as often—through changing the material—varying the elements of the effect. The results can be infinitely different—the result can be splitting a stone—a hole for gunpowder—a statue etc.

Thus on the one hand, every tool modifies the powers and thoughts of the artist that conduct it to the material, and conversely—it modifies the effects of resistance of the material that conduct it to the artist.

74.   Anyone who could use a chisel to paint, make music etc., in short, who could work magic—would not need the chisel—the chisel would be superfluous. Moreover a magic wand could also be an indirect tool.

75.   All discharge of energy is instantaneous—transient. Enduring energy is matter. All energy appears only *as it passes*.

76.   To the extent that a thing exists for me—I am its purpose—it refers to me—it exists for my sake. My will determines me—and thus also my property. The world is to be as I will it. Originally the world is as I will it— thus if I do not find it so then I must seek the error of this product in both factors—or in one. Either the world is a degenerate world—or my contra-

dictory will is not my true will—or both at once are indistinguishably true at once. Degenerate self—degenerate world. *Restoration.*

77. Everything mystical is personal—accordingly it is an elementary variation of the universe.

78. All conviction is independent of natural truth—it refers to magical or miraculous truth. One can only be convinced of natural truth—to the extent that it becomes miraculous truth. All proof rests on conviction, and is accordingly only a makeshift where comprehensive miraculous truth is lacking. Therefore all natural truths rest equally on miraculous truth.

79. The act of transcending oneself is the highest in every respect—the point of origin—the *genesis of life.* Thus the flame is nothing but such an act. Thus all philosophy begins where philosophizing philosophizes itself[18]—that is, where it at once consumes (determines, compels) and renews again (does not determine, releases). The history of this process is philosophy. Thus all living morality begins at the point at which out of virtue I act against virtue—then the life of virtue begins, through which perhaps its capacity increases infinitely, without ever losing its boundary—that is, the condition of the possibility of its *life.*

80. All despair is deterministic—but even determinism is an *element* of the philosophical universe or system. The isolation of the elements and false belief in their reality is the source of most, perhaps all, errors hitherto.

81. Every person who sets himself apart and usually seems affected is after all a person in whom a principle is stirring. Every unnatural way of behaving is a symptom of a maxim that has become crystallized. Independence must begin affectedly. All morality begins affectedly. It demands affectation. Every beginning is awkward.

82. In order to give a conversation a desired direction it is only necessary to hold fast to the goal. Thus one approaches the goal gradually, for its power of attraction is becoming active. Through this attention to a heterogeneous thought the wittiest transitions often arise, the nicest connections. One is often there more quickly than one thinks.

83. Language too is a product of the organic drive for development. Now as the latter everywhere forms the same product under the most diverse circumstances, so here too through civilization, through a rising level of development and vivification, language is formed into the most profound expression of the idea of organism, into the system of philosophy.

All language is a postulate. It has a positive, free origin. One must agree to think of certain things at certain signs, to construct something definite within oneself intentionally.

84. Whoever first understood how to count to two, even if he still found it difficult to keep on counting, saw nonetheless the possibility of infinite counting according to the same laws.

85. The possibility of philosophy rests on the possibility of producing thoughts according to rules—of thinking truly communally—the art of collaboration in philosophy. If communal thought is possible, so also communal will is possible, the realization of great, new ideas.

86. Only what is incomplete can be comprehended—can take us further. What is complete is only enjoyed. If we want to comprehend nature we must postulate it as incomplete, to reach an unknown variable in this way. All determination is relative.

87. To become a human being is an art.

88. All memory is the present. In the purer element all memory would appear to us like the necessary preliminary to poetry.

89. The lyric poem is for heroes, it creates heroes. The epic poem is for ordinary people. The hero is lyrical, the ordinary person epic, the genius dramatic—man is lyrical, woman epic, marriage dramatic.

90. The perfect person should be a beautiful satire, capable of giving anything any desired form, of filling each form with the most diverse life and moving it.

91. Every person has his own language. Language is the expression of the spirit. Individual languages. Language genius. Skill in translating into and out of other languages. Richness and euphony of every language. True expression makes a clear idea. Just as soon as one has the right name one has the ideas as well. Transparent, leading expression.

92. Everything must become food. The art of drawing life out of everything. To vivify everything is the goal of life. Pleasure is life. The absence of pleasure is a way to pleasure, as death is a way to life.

93. The most commonplace thing expressed in true euphony is worth perpetual contemplation. In foreign languages one feels in a more lively fashion that each speech act ought to be a composition. People are much

too careless in speaking and writing. Ideal speech is part of the realization of the ideal world.

94.   The key to life lies in intellectual contemplation.

95.   The Last Day is the synthesis of present life and death (of life after death).

96.   Only an artist can divine the meaning of life.

97.   Image—not allegory, not symbol of something other than itself: symbol of itself.

98.   Philosophy is not supposed to explain nature but rather to explain itself. All satisfaction is dissolution of the self. Need arises through division—influence from outside—injury. It must regain its balance. The self-dissolution of instinct, this self-immolation of illusion, of the illusory problem, is precisely the voluptuous quality in the satisfaction of instinct. What is life otherwise? Despair, fear of death, is one of the most interesting deceptions of just this kind. It begins sthenically, as in the tragedy, it ends asthenically and precisely as such it becomes a satisfying feeling—a pulsebeat of our emotional life. It can also begin asthenically and end sthenically. It is all one. A tragedy which leaves too much melancholy behind has not begun sthenically enough. Every story contains life, a problem which dissolves itself. Thus each life is a story.
Hamlet ends very well: it begins asthenically, it ends sthenically. *Meister* ends with the synthesis of the antinomies, because it is written for and by the understanding.

99.   Whoever sees life other than as a self-destroying illusion is himself still preoccupied with life.
Life must not be a novel that is given to us, but one that is made by us.

100. Everything is seed.

3 *Logological Fragments II*

1.   The first human being is the first spirit-seer.[1] Everything appears to him as spirit. What are children other than first human beings? The fresh gaze of the child is more brimming with emotion than the intuition of the most determined seer.

2.   The siesta of the realm of spirits is the flower world. In India people are still slumbering, and their sacred dream is a garden flowing with milk and honey.[2]

3.   It is only because of the weakness of our organs and of our contact with ourselves that we do not discover ourselves to be in a fairy world. All fairy tales are only dreams of that familiar world of home which is everywhere and nowhere. The higher powers in us, which one day will carry out our will like genies, are now muses that refresh us with sweet memories along this arduous path.

4.   Sculpture, music, and poetry relate to each other as do epic, lyric, and drama. They are inseparable elements, which in each free art entity are bound together, and only as their own nature allows, in different relations.

5.   What is a human being? A perfect trope of the spirit. All true communication thus has symbolic character—and so are not caresses true communications?

6.   A beam of light breaks up into something quite different, as well as into colors. At least the beam of light is capable of being animated, at

which the soul then breaks up into soul colors.³ Who is not reminded of the glance of his beloved?

7.   Every spiritual touch is like the touch of a magic wand. Everything can become the tool of magic. But whoever thinks the effects of such touch are so fabulous, whoever finds the effects of a magic spell so marvelous, need only remind himself of the first touch of his beloved's hand, her first meaningful glance, where the magic wand is the detached beam of light, the first kiss, the first word of love, and ask himself whether the spell and magic of these moments is not also fabulous and wondrous, indissoluble and eternal?

8.   Humanity is the higher meaning of our planet, the nerve that connects this part of it with the upper world, the eye it raises to heaven.

9.   The philosopher lives on problems as the human being does on food. An insoluble problem is an indigestible food. What spice is to food, the paradoxical is to problems. A problem is truly solved when it is destroyed as such. So it is with food. In both cases the gain is the activity aroused by both. However, as there is nourishing food there are also nourishing problems, whose elements become an increase in my intelligence. But through doing philosophy, to the extent that it is an absolute operation, as well as being ceaselessly renewed my intelligence is also continually being improved—which with food only takes place up to a certain moment. A rapid improvement in our intelligence is of as much concern as a sudden increase in strength. The right pace in health and getting well is slow—even if here too there are different grades of speed as there are different constitutions. Thus as little as one eats in order to acquire novel, strange substances—one does philosophy equally little in order to find novel, strange truths. One does philosophy for just the same reason that one is alive. If one should manage some time to live without given foods, so too one will manage to do philosophy without given problems, if some are not even at this stage already.

10.   We know and do really only what we want to know and do. The difficulty is only to find this. Exact observation of the first moment, as the hint appears like the germ of an idea, will convince us that everything is already there within it and is only developed and clarified afterwards.

11.   Witty, significant, sentimental, moral, scholarly, political, historical, descriptive, individual, funny or ridiculous, artistic, humorous, Romantic, tragic, poetic anecdotes.⁴

History is a great anecdote. An anecdote is a historical element—a historical molecule or epigram. A history in anecdotes—Voltaire did something of the kind—is an extremely interesting work of art. History in its usual form is a series of anecdotes that have been welded together or have flowed into each other in a continuum.

Which is preferable, the continuous or the discrete? A great individual or a crowd of small individuals? The former is infinite—the latter is specific, finite, fixed, determinate.

A master of anecdotes must know how to turn everything into anecdotes. Schlegel is right, the true novel must be a satire.[5]

Something like Lichtenberg's commentary on Hogarth could be written about *Wilhelm Meister*.[6] Up to now a review was supposed to be the complete essence and extract of what could be written and said about a book—and even methodical and systematic as well. We have not come nearly as far as that. If it only were a satire at least. This demand should first be divided into various components. Like everything else, a book engenders a thousand sensations and functions—determinate, specific, and free.

12.   A large class of anecdotes are those which show a human trait in a strange, striking way, for example, cunning, magnanimity, bravery, inconstancy, bizarrerie, cruelty, wit, imagination, benevolence, morality, love, friendship, wisdom, narrow-mindedness etc. In short, it is a gallery of many kinds of human actions, an anatomy of humanity. They are anecdotes for the study of man and therefore didactic. Another large class includes those which produce an effect, which are meant to engage our imagination in a pleasing way. They could perhaps in general be called poetic anecdotes, even if only very few of them are beautiful (absolute) poetry.

Thus we would have two main classes, descriptive and poetic anecdotes. The former employ our cognitive capacity, the latter our capacity for desire.

The art of telling anecdotes. A true anecdote is of itself already poetic. It occupies the imagination. Is not the imagination, or the higher organ, the poetic sense altogether? It is only not pure poetry if the imagination is aroused for the sake of the understanding or the cognitive capacity. A witty anecdote consists in arousing attentiveness, tension, and excitement or nonexcitement. The last class includes all deceptive anecdotes.

Descriptive anecdotes refer to an interesting subject, their interest only relates to something outside, the purely poetic anecdote refers to itself, it is interesting for its own sake.

13.   The novel is about life—represents *life*. It would be theatrical only in relation to the poet. Often it contains the incidents of a masquerade— a masked incident among masked characters. If the mask is lifted—they are familiar incidents—familiar characters. The novel as such contains no definite result—it is not the image or fact of a *proposition*. It is the visible execution—the realization of an idea. But an idea cannot be comprehended in a proposition. An idea is an *infinite series* of propositions—an *irrational number*—it *cannot be set* (to music)—incommensurable. Ought not all irrationality to be relative?
But the law of its continuation can be laid down—and criticism of a novel should be undertaken according to this law.

14.   *The *dithyramb* among physical actions is the *embrace*. Hence it must be judged according to its natural laws.

15.   Judgment—product and object of the sense of the senses—of the general sense.
   * The story—a maximum of the poetic, popular representation of the philosophy of the first period[7]—or of philosophy in a state of nature—of the detached philosophemes of the first civilization or *formation*—not pure original poetry—but artificial—philosophy that has become poetry. It does not belong to fine art—it is technical—the product of intention— the conductor of a purpose. Hence the intentional freedom in the choice of material—material that is compelled betrays *intention*—the plan of a rational being.
For this age reason and the divine spirit do not speak audibly or strikingly enough from a human being—stones, trees, animals must speak in order to make the human being feel himself and make himself reflect.
The first art is the study of hieroglyphs.[8]
Then the art of communication and reflection, or language, and the art of representation and shaping, or poetry, are still one. Not until later does this raw mass divide—then the art of naming arises, language in the true sense—philosophy—and fine art, creative art, poetry itself.
The wisdom of riddles, or the art of concealing the substance under its own characteristics—of mystically confusing its features, belongs in this period as practice for the ingenuity of youth. Mystical, allegorical words may have been the beginning of this popularization of the earliest theo-

rems—if indeed knowledge itself did not come straight into the world in this popular form. Parables are a much later formation. Artificial or technical poetry in general includes rhetorical poetry. The character of artificial poetry is purposiveness—it is directed toward the outside. Language in the most authentic sense belongs in the sphere of artificial poetry. Its purpose is specific communication. Thus if one wants to call language—expression of an intention, then all artificial poetry is language—its purpose is specific communication—arousal of *specific* thought.

The novel belongs to the category of *natural poetry*—the allegory to that of the artificial.[9]

Natural poetry can often have the appearance of the artificial—the *didactic*—without suffering any harm. But it must be connected to it only by chance, only freely. This appearance of allegory then gives it yet another stimulus—and it cannot have enough forms of stimulus (excitements of all kinds).

Music—sculpture, and poetry are synonyms.

16.   *Ordinary stories with their morals are like pictures beneath which the artist must write what they are supposed to mean.

17.   *As the painter sees visible objects with quite different eyes from those of the common person—so too the poet experiences the events of the outer and the inner world very differently from the ordinary person. But nowhere is it more striking than in music—that it is only the spirit that poeticizes the objects and the changes of the material, and that the beautiful, the subject of art, is not given to us nor can it be found ready in phenomena. All sounds produced by nature are rough—and empty of spirit—only the musical soul often finds the rustling of the forest—the whistling of the wind, the song of the nightingale, the babbling of the brook melodious and meaningful. The musician takes the essence of his art from within himself—not even the slightest suspicion of imitation can apply to him. To the painter, visible nature seems everywhere to be doing his preliminary work—to be entirely his unattainable model. But really the painter's art has arisen just as independently, quite as a priori, as the musician's. Only the painter uses an infinitely more difficult *symbolic language* than the musician—the painter really paints with his eye—his art is the art of seeing with order and beauty. Here seeing is quite active—entirely a formative activity. His image is only his secret sign—his expression—his reproducing tool. Suppose we compare the written musical *note* with this artificial sign. The musician might rather counter the

painter's image with the diverse movements of the fingers, the feet, and the mouth. Really the musician too hears actively—he distinguishes by hearing. For most people this reversed use of the senses is certainly a mystery, but every artist will be more or less clearly aware of it. Almost every person is to a limited degree already an artist. In fact he sees actively and not passively—he feels actively and not passively. The main difference is this: the artist has vivified the germ of self-formative life in his sense organs—he has raised the excitability of these *for the spirit* and is thereby able to allow ideas to flow out of them at will—without external prompting—to use them as tools for such modifications of the real world *as he will.* On the other hand for the nonartist they speak only through the intervention of external prompting, and the spirit, like inert matter, seems to be governed by or to submit to the constraint of the basic laws of mechanics, namely that all changes presuppose an external cause and that effect and countereffect must equal each other at all times. At least it is some consolation to know that this mechanical behavior is unnatural to the spirit and is *transient,* like all that is spiritually unnatural.

Yet even with the most humble person the spirit does not wholly obey the law of mechanics—and hence it would be possible for everyone to develop this higher propensity and skill of the organ.

But to come back to the differences between painting and music, what is immediately striking is that in music sign, tool, and material are separate, but in painting they are one, and just for this reason in the latter each element *in abstracto* appears so incomplete. So much can be established with certainty from this, it seems to me, namely that painting is far more *difficult* than music. That it is as it were one step closer to the holy place of the spirit and therefore nobler than music, if I may put it that way, may well be inferred from just that usual encomiastic argument of the admirers of music, that music exercises a much stronger and more general effect. This physical quantity ought not to be the yardstick of the intellectual stature of the arts, and would be rather a contraindication of it. Even animals know music and have it themselves—but they have no idea of painting. They would really not see the most beautiful scene or the most charming picture. A painted object from the circle of their acquaintance only deceives them—but qua picture they have no sensation of it.

A good actor is indeed a tangible and poetic instrument. Opera and ballet are indeed tangible poetic concerts—cooperative works of art employing several tangible instruments. The active sense of feeling. *Poetry.*

18.   *The ideal of morality has no more dangerous rival than the ideal of the greatest strength—of the most vigorous life—what has also been called the ideal of aesthetic greatness, really quite rightly although it is commonly held to be quite wrong. This is barbaric to the maximum degree—and unhappily in these days of cultural degeneracy has gathered very many supporters precisely among the greatest weaklings. Through this ideal the human being becomes an animal-spirit—a mixture whose brutal wit has just such brutal power of attraction for weaklings.

19.   *Morality and philosophy are arts. The first is the art of being able to choose appropriately between the motives behind the actions of a moral or artistic idea a priori, thereby endowing all actions with great, profound meaning—the art of giving life a higher meaning and in this way of skill-fully ordering the mass of internal and external actions (internal ones are attitudes and decisions) in an ideal whole and uniting them. The second is the art of dealing with thoughts in a similar way, of choosing between thoughts—the art of producing all our conceptions according to an absolute, artistic idea and of developing the thought of a world system a priori out of the depths of our spirit—to use the faculty of thought actively—to represent a purely intelligible world.

The art of becoming a philosopher lies in method. The art of becoming a moral person—in *ascetics*.

Actually in all true arts one idea—one spirit—is realized, is produced from within—the world of spirits. For the eye it is the visible world a priori—for the ear the audible world a priori—for the moral organ the moral world a priori—for the organ of thought the conceivable world a priori and so on. All these worlds are only different expressions of different tools of one spirit and its world.

20.   *The world of books is indeed only a caricature of the real world. Both spring from the same source—but the former appears in a freer, more flexible medium. Hence all colors are sharper there—fewer shades in between—the movements more lively—the outlines hence more strik-ing—the expression extravagant. The former appears only in *fragmentary form*—the latter is *whole*. Therefore, the former is more poetic—more inspired—more interesting—more picturesque—but also more untrue—more unphilosophical—more immoral. Most people, including most scholars, have also only a book view—a fragmentary view of the real world—and then it suffers from the same faults but also enjoys the same advantages as the book world. Many books are also nothing but represen-

tations of such individual, fragmentary views of the real world. More about the relation of the book world (literary world) to the real world.

21.   *Most people do not themselves know how interesting they really are, what interesting things they really say. A true representation of themselves—a sketch and assessment of what they say would evoke the greatest amazement in them about themselves and help them to discover in themselves a completely new world.

Writers are as one-sided as all artists of one kind—only even more stubborn. Among professional writers there are strikingly few liberal people—especially when they have no other subsistence at all but their writing. To live by writing is a highly risky undertaking, even for genuine spiritual education and freedom.

22.   *With all the gaps and imperfections in his knowledge which necessarily arise from the nature of his study, a self-educated person nonetheless has the great advantage that every new idea he acquires is at once taken up into the community of his knowledge and ideas, and blends with the whole in the closest way, which then provides the opportunity for original combinations and all kinds of new discoveries.

23.   *The calmer—the more agile—the spirit wants to be—the more it must seek at the same time to occupy the body in an *insignificant* way. It is as it were the negative chain which it drops on the ground in order to be the more active and effective. Music—food, or any means of stimulation—beautiful pictures for the eye—odors—rubbing—or walking around.

24.   That individual will be the most perfect and *purely systematic*, who is individualized only by a *single absolute chance*—for example, by his birth. In this chance all his other chance incidents, the infinite series of his circumstances, must lie one within the other or, better still, be determined as his chance incidents or circumstances. Derivation of an individual life from a single chance—a single arbitrary act.

Breaking up of one chance incident—one great arbitrary act, into many—into infinitely many—through gradual absorption—slow, successive penetration—happening.

*A novel writer performs a kind of *bouts rimés*[10]—when he makes a well-ordered, regular series out of a given number of chance incidents and situations—and leads an individual for a single purpose through all these incidents in a purposeful way. He needs a special individual who determines the events and is determined by them. This change, or the variations in one individual—in a *continuous* series constitute the interesting material of a novel.

25. Organs of their nature have no tendency to be determining and fixed—or to combine to form one individual body—it is only through the spirit that they acquire common central points—and through this they are obliged to perform certain regular, immutable functions. In this way, where the hand feels and the ear hears, the eye must form a particular color and a particular, suitable outline and vice versa. Without spirit there are no colors and outlines—no different sounds etc.—no different feelings and particular surfaces and boundaries etc. Every body is held together and determined by a *monad*.

26. *In the same way as we move our mental organ at will—modify its movement at will—observe this and its products—and express them in diverse ways—in the same way as we articulate the movements of our mental organ—as we externalize them in gestures—give them form in action, as in general we move and behave freely—combine and separate our movements—in just the same way we must also move the inner organs of our bodies, constrain them, combine and separate them, *learn* them. Our whole body is fully capable of being moved by the spirit at will. The effects of fear, terror—sadness, anger—envy—shame, joy, imagination etc. are sufficient indications. Besides there are enough examples of people—who have achieved voluntary mastery over individual parts of their body which are usually not under the control of the will. Then everyone will be his own doctor—and will be able to feel his body in a complete, sure, and exact way. Then for the first time the human being will be truly independent of nature, perhaps even in a position to restore lost limbs, to kill himself merely by his will, and thereby to achieve for the first time true insight into the body—mind—world, life—death and the world of spirits. Perhaps then it will only rest with him to quicken inert matter. He will compel his senses *to produce* for him the shape he demands—and he will be able to live in *his* world in the truest sense. Then he will be capable of separating himself from his body—if he finds it good to do so. He will see, hear—and feel—what, how and in whichever combination he will.

Fichte taught—and discovered—the active use of the mental organ. Has Fichte perhaps discovered the laws of the active use of the organs in general. Intellectual perception is nothing else.

27.   What is nature? An encyclopedic systematic index or plan of our spirit. Why should we be content with the mere catalogue of our treasures—let us examine them for ourselves—and work with them and use them in diverse ways.

*The fate which oppresses us is the inertia of our spirit. Through extending and cultivating our activity we shall transform ourselves into fate.

Everything seems to stream inward into us, because we do not stream outward. We are negative because we want to be—the more positive we become, the more negative will the world around us become—until at last there will be no more negation—but instead we are all in all.

God wants there to be gods.

*Is not our body in itself nothing but a common central effect of our senses—if we have mastery over our senses—if we are able to transform them into activity at will—to center them at a common point, then it only depends on us—to give ourselves the body we want.

Indeed, if our senses are nothing other than modifications of the mental organ—of the *absolute element*—then with mastery over this element we shall also be able to modify and direct our senses as we please.

28.   *To some extent the painter already has the eye—the musician the ear—the poet the imaginative power—the speech organ, and the sensation—or rather several organs at once—whose effects he combines and directs toward the speech organ or toward the hand—(the philosopher is the absolute organ)—in his *power—and is active through them at will*, he represents the world of spirits through them at will. Genius is nothing but spirit in this active use of the organs. Up to now we have *had* only single *genius*—but the spirit is to become total *genius*.

Fichte has only now begun to realize a single idea in this way—*the idea of a mental system*. Thus whoever wishes to participate in this idea—must imitate him in it—of course through *independent activity* according to *this idea*. The idea must contain the complete *law of its own dissolution*.

29.   *One person succeeded—he lifted the veil of the goddess at Saïs—But what did he see? he saw—wonder of wonders—himself.[11]

30.   *Rule*—specification of direction and measurement—model, design, sketch of particular directions, and relations.

Ideas—free designs, models, projections of genius.

Art—the capacity to produce in determined and free ways—*determined*—according to a *determined* rule—to an idea that has already been determined from outside, which we call concept—undetermined, according to an authentic, pure idea.

31.   Art breaks up, if you will, into *real*, completed, successful art, which is effective by means of the *external* organs (conductors)—and *imaginary* art, which as it proceeds is retained in the internal organs (*insulated* by the internal organs, as nonconductors) and is only effective by means of these. The latter is called science in the broadest sense.

Both of these divide into two main categories—into determinate art, which is *guided* by objects—or other central functions of the senses, is determined by concepts, finite, limited, mediated art—and indeterminate art, free, unmediated, original, not derived, cyclical, beautiful, independent, realizing pure ideas—art that is vivified by pure ideas.

The former is only the means to an end—the latter is an end in itself, a satisfying activity of the spirit, *self-enjoyment* of the spirit.

Science in the broadest sense is what is pursued by scholars—masters of determinate art—and philosophers are masters of indeterminate, free art. Art *kat exochen*, or real (external) art is pursued by craftsmen—masters of the determinate part—and by artists *kat exochen*, masters of the free category.

The scholar attains the maximum in his field through the highest simplification—of the rules and therefore also of the subject matter. If he can derive all determinate rules from one *determinate* rule—reduce all determinate ends to one end etc., then he has brought his field to the highest degree of its perfection. The encyclopedic scholar, who does this within the compass of all determinate sciences—and so transforms all determinate sciences into one determinate science, is the maximum of a scholar. One could call determinate art a science in the narrower sense. The same with the philosopher.

One can call philosophy the free, imaginary art. The philosopher who in his philosophy can transform all single philosophemes into a single one—who can make one whole out of all single instances of these, attains the maximum in his philosophy. He attains the maximum of a philosopher if he combines all philosophies into a single philosophy.

It is the same with craftsmen and artists.

32.   The scholar and the craftsman proceed mechanically in their simplification. They combine disparate forces—and methodically disperse this combined force and direction again. The philosopher and the artist proceed *organically*—if I may describe it so—they combine freely by

means of a pure idea and separate according to a free idea. Their principle—their idea of combining—is an organic germ—which develops and shapes itself freely into a form which contains indeterminate individuals and is infinitely *individual* and capable of being cultivated in any way—an idea rich in ideas.

33.   Individual original form—characters of my *original will*. Character, from *instinct*—character, from *principles*. *The more it is dependent on chance and circumstances—the less I have a determinate, cultivated—*applied* will. The more it has these qualities, the more it is independent in those respects.
The art of becoming omnipotent—the art of realizing our will totally. We must attain power over the body as we do over the mind. The body is the tool to shape and modify the world—we must therefore seek to cultivate our bodies to become an organ *capable of anything*. Modification of our tool is modification of the world.

34.   *The public is an infinitely large, diverse, interesting person—a mysterious person of infinite worth—the actual absolute stimulus of the artist.

35.   *Finding an idea—that is, distinguishing it among several feelings in the external world by feeling—from several perspectives by seeing—from several experiences and facts by experiencing—seeking out—the right thought from several thoughts—distinguishing, thinking out the tool of the idea. This requires a *physiognomical* sense of the diverse *expressions*, tools of the idea. I must understand the art of reasoning from the idea to its appearance.

36.   *Language to the second power. For example, a story is the expression of a whole thought—and belongs in the study of hieroglyphs of the second power—to the *language of sound and symbol* squared. It has poetic merits and is not *rhetorical*—subaltern—if it is a perfect expression—if it is *euphonic* squared—correct and precise—if it is like an *extra expression* for the sake of the expression—at least if it does not appear as a vehicle—but is in itself a perfect product of the *higher organ* of language. Language in the true sense is *the function of a tool as such. Every tool expresses, is given its stamp by* the idea of its user.
If one organ serves another then it is, so to speak, its *tongue*—its throat, its mouth. The tool that serves the spirit most willingly and is capable most

easily of diverse modifications becomes primarily its language tool—hence we have language of the mouth and the fingers.

37. *We know something only—in so far as we *express* it—that is, in so far as we can *make* it. The more perfectly and variously we can *produce* something, *execute it*, the better we *know* it. We know it perfectly if we can *communicate* it, arouse it everywhere and in all ways—if we can produce an individual *expression* of it in each organ.

38. Our states are almost nothing but *legal* institutions—only *defensive* organizations. Unfortunately they are not educational institutions—academies—and art societies, at least only very inadequately. Thus people must supplement this through special coalitions. One should seek to replace missing police institutions too through private societies.

39. A marriage is a political epigram. The epigram is only an elementary poetic form of expression—a poetic element—a primitive poem.

40. Centripetal force is the synthetic striving of the spirit—centrifugal force the analytical striving of the spirit. Striving toward unity—striving towards diversity. Through the mutual determination of each by the other—that higher synthesis of unity and diversity itself will be produced—whereby one is in all and all in one.

41. *Poetry is the hero of philosophy. Philosophy raises poetry to the status of a principle. It teaches us to recognize the worth of poetry. Philosophy is *the theory* of *poetry*. It shows us what poetry is, that it is one and all.

42. The dabbler does not know in any art what it is all about—he imitates like a monkey—and has no sense of the essential core of art. The true painter etc. certainly can distinguish the picturesque from the unpicturesque everywhere. So it is with the poet, the novelist, the travel writer. The writer of chronicles is the dabbler in history—he wants to give everything and gives nothing. So it is throughout. Every art has its *individual* sphere—he who does not know this exactly or have a sense of it—will never be an artist.

43. *The magician is a poet. The prophet is to the magician as the man of taste is to the poet.

44.   *Having something made and enjoying it seems indeed more noble than *completing* and *producing*—watching—than doing—thinking, than realizing, or being!!!!

45.   *Body, mind, and spirit are the elements of the world—as epic, lyric, and drama are those of the poem.

46.   *The true poet is *all-knowing*—he is a real world in miniature.

47.   *A definition is a *real*, or generating name. A normal name is only a note.

48.   *Shem hamephorash—name of the name.[12] The real definition is a magic word. Each idea has a scale of names—the top one is absolute and unnameable. Toward the middle the names become more common and in the end turn into antithetical names—the highest of which is again nameless.

49.   On nature, as a *closed body*—as *a tree*—on which we are the *blossom* buds.
Natures, on the one hand, are beings—such that the whole serves the *parts*—that the parts are ends in themselves—the parts are independent. With persons, on the other hand—the contrary relation obtains. Where both mutually necessitate the other and each or rather none is an end in itself, these are intermediate beings between nature and person. These are the extremes, which are connected by various middle parts.

50.   Everything that is *lovable* is an object (a thing)—that which is infinitely lovable is an infinite thing—something one can have only by ceaseless, infinite activity. One can only possess a thing.

51.   The clever leaders of the French have achieved a master stroke by being able to give their war the appearance of a war of opinions.[13] It has been this only in cabinets of speculation and in very few places and individuals—and then only additionally, not in the first place.

52.   *At any event the world is the result of a mutual effect between myself and the *divine being*. Everything that exists and comes into being—does so out of contact between spirits.

53.   External prompting takes place only when the self is deficient in making itself heterogeneous internally—and in touching itself!!!!

54.　Everything we experience is a *communication*. Thus the world is indeed a *communication*—a revelation of the spirit. The age has passed when the spirit of God could be understood. The meaning of the world is lost. We have stopped at the letter. As a result of the appearance we have lost that which is appearing. Formulary beings.

55.　As one progresses so much becomes dispensable—much appears in a different light—so that I should not have wished to work on a single point before the exposition of the great, *all-transforming idea*.[14] That which is imperfect appears most tolerably as a fragment—and thus this form of communication is to be recommended above that which as a whole is not yet finished—and yet has single noteworthy opinions to offer.

56.　From a higher point of view, untruth has a much worse side than the usual one. It is the foundation of a *false world*—the foundation of a chain of errors and confusions that cannot be undone. Untruth is the source of all wickedness and evil. *Absolute positing* of the false. Eternal error. One untruth gives birth to countless others. An absolutely posited untruth is so infinitely difficult to expunge.

4   *Monologue*

There is really something very foolish about speaking and writing; proper conversation is merely a word game.[1] One can only marvel at the ridiculous mistake that people make when they think—that they speak for the sake of things. The particular quality of language, the fact that it is concerned only with itself, is known to no one.[2] Language is such a marvelous and fruitful secret—because when someone speaks merely for the sake of speaking, he utters the most splendid, most original truths. But if he wants to speak about something definite, capricious language makes him say the most ridiculous and confused stuff. This is also the cause of the hatred that so many serious people feel toward language. They notice its mischief, but not the fact that the chattering they scorn is the infinitely serious aspect of language. If one could only make people understand that it is the same with language as with mathematical formulae. These constitute a world of their own. They play only with themselves, express nothing but their own marvelous nature, and just for this reason they are so expressive—just for this reason the strange play of relations between things is mirrored in them. Only through their freedom are they elements of nature and only in their free movements does the world soul manifest itself in them and make them a sensitive measure and ground plan of things. So it is too with language—on the one hand, anyone who is sensitive to its fingering, its rhythm, its musical spirit, who perceives within himself the delicate working of its inner nature, and moves his tongue or his hand accordingly, will be a prophet; on the other hand, anyone who knows how to write truths like these but does not have ear and sense enough for it will be outwitted by language itself and mocked by people as

Cassandra was by the Trojans. Even if in saying this I believe I have described the essence and function of poetry in the clearest possible way, at the same time I know that no one can understand it, and I have said something quite foolish because I wanted to say it, and in this way no poetry comes about. What would it be like though if I had to speak? and this instinct of language to speak were the hallmark of what inspires language, of the efficacy of language within me? and were my will to want only everything that I was obliged to do, in the end could this be poetry without my knowledge or belief and could it make a secret of language understandable? and thus I would be a born writer, for a writer is surely only a language enthusiast?

5   Faith and Love or The King and Queen

1.   If in a large mixed company one wants to speak about something secret with just a few people, and one is not sitting next to them, one must speak in a special language.[1] This special language can be a foreign language in either *sound* or *images*. The latter kind will be a language of tropes and riddles.

2.   Many people have thought that in speaking about delicate, easily abused subjects one should use learned language, for example, one should write in Latin about things of that kind. It would depend on seeing whether one could not speak in the ordinary national language so that only *he* who was meant to understand it could understand. Every true secret must of itself exclude the profane. Whoever understands it is of himself, by right, *an initiate.*

3.   Mystical expression is one more stimulus to thought. All truth is ancient. The stimulus of novelty lies only in variety of expression. The more contrast in its forms, the greater the pleasure of recognition.

4.   One finds what one loves everywhere, and sees similarities everywhere. The greater the love the more extensive and manifold is this similar world. My beloved is the abbreviation of the universe, the universe is the extension of my beloved. To the lover of learning, all its branches offer garlands and remembrances for his beloved.

5.   But where do these solemn, mystical-political philosophemes come from? An enthusiast expresses his higher life in all his functions; thus he does philosophy *more poetically* as well, and in a livelier manner than

usual. This deep tone too is part of the symphony of his powers and faculties. But does not the general gain by its relations with the individual, and the individual by its relations with the general?

6.   Let the dragonflies go; they are innocent *strangers*
      Who follow the twin stars joyfully, with gifts, to this place.[2]

7.   A blooming country is surely a more royal work of art than a park. A tasteful park is an English invention. A country that satisfies heart and mind might well become a German invention; and the inventor would surely be the king of all inventors.

8.   The best of all the former French monarchs had resolved to make his subjects so prosperous that each of them could have a chicken with rice on his table every Sunday.[3] Would not that government be more desirable under which the peasant preferred to eat a piece of moldy bread at home rather than roast meat in another country, and thanked God heartily for the good fortune to have been born in this country?

9.   If I were to become a prince tomorrow I should first ask the king for a eudiometer like his.[4] No instrument is more necessary for a prince. I should also, as he does, seek to draw the air for my state from blooming plantations rather than from saltpeter.

10.   Gold and silver are the blood of the state. If the heart and head are too full of blood, that betrays weakness in them both. The stronger the heart is, the more vigorously and generously it will pump blood to the extremities. Each limb is warm and alive, and the blood flows swiftly and strongly back to the heart.

11.   A collapsing throne is like a falling mountain, which shatters the plain and leaves behind a dead sea where there once was a fertile land and a joyful dwelling place.[5]

12.   You have only to level the mountains and the sea will thank you for it. The sea is the element of liberty and equality. Still it warns against stepping on a bed of firestone; otherwise the volcano will show itself and with it the germ of a new continent.[6]

13.   The noxious vapors of the moral world behave differently from their namesakes in nature. The former rise readily into the air, while the latter stay on the ground. For the dweller on the heights there is no better remedy for such vapors than flowers and sunshine. These last have only rarely

coincided on the heights. But on one of the loftiest moral heights on earth one can now enjoy the purest air and see a lily in the sun.[7]

14.   It was no wonder if for the most part the mountaintops just thundered down into the valleys and laid the plains to waste. Evil clouds usually gathered about them, and hid from them the place where they rose out of the land; then the plain appeared to them only like a dark abyss across which the clouds seemed to be carrying them, or like a rebellious sea, since nothing was really rising up against them and gradually blunting them and washing them away other than the seemingly devoted clouds.

15.   A true royal couple is for the whole human being what a constitution is for the intellect alone. One can only be interested in a constitution as one is in a letter for its own sake. If the sign is neither a beautiful image nor a song, then devotion to signs is the most perverse of all inclinations.[8] What is a law if it is not the expression of the will of a beloved person who is worthy of our respect? Does not the mystical sovereign need a symbol, like every idea, and what symbol is more estimable and more appropriate than a gracious, excellent person? Brevity of expression is after all worth something, and is not a human being a briefer, more beautiful expression of a spirit than a company? Whoever is rich in spirit is not constrained by limits and differences; rather he is stimulated by them. Only he who is without spirit feels burdened and constrained. Moreover, a born king is also better than one who is made. The best of people will not be able to support an elevation of this kind without being altered. He who is born so is not overcome by giddiness, he is not excessively stimulated by such a situation. And in the end, is not birth the original kind of choice? Those who question the freedom of this choice or the unanimity of making it must never have felt life stirring within themselves.
Anyone who comes along with his historical experiences does not know at all what I am talking about nor the point of view from which I am talking; to him I am speaking Arabic, and it would be the best thing for him to go on his way and not mix with listeners whose idiom and local speech are quite alien to him.

16.   As far as I am concerned it may well be time for the letter to have its turn. It is no great praise of our age to say that it is so far removed from nature, so lacking in meaning for family life, so disinclined for the most beautiful, poetic form of society. How amazed our cosmopolites would be if the age of eternal peace appeared before them and they beheld the

highest, most cultivated form of humanity in the form of the monarchy?[9] Then the paper gum which sticks people together would turn to dust, and the spirit would frighten away those ghosts that appeared in its stead in lifeless letters and issued in shreds from pens and presses, and would blend all humanity together like a pair of lovers.

17.   The king is the pure life principle of the state; he is exactly the same as the sun in the solar system. It follows that the highest form of life in the state, the sphere of light, first comes into being around the life principle. It is to a greater or lesser extent buried like ore in every citizen of the state. The utterances of the citizen in the vicinity of the king hence will become brilliant, and as poetic as possible, or they will be the expression of the highest animation. But since the spirit is at the same time at its most effective while in the highest animation, and since the actions of the spirit are reflections, but reflection of its nature is formative and therefore the beautiful or perfect reflection is linked with the highest animation, then the expression of the citizen of the state in the vicinity of the king will be expression of the highest, most restrained fullness of energy, expression of the liveliest stirrings, subject to the most respectful attentiveness, a kind of behavior which is susceptible to being regulated. No court can survive without etiquette. But there is a natural etiquette, the beautiful kind, and an artificial, modish, ugly kind. Production of the first will thus be a not unimportant concern of the intelligent king, since it has a significant influence on taste and devotion to the form of monarchy.

18.   Every citizen of the state is a servant of the state. He receives his income only as such. It is very wrong to call the king the first servant of the state. The king is not a citizen of the state, it follows that he is also not a servant of the state. The distinguishing character of the monarchy lies precisely in the fact of belief in a higher-born person, of voluntary acceptance of an ideal person. I cannot choose a leader among my peers; I can entrust nothing to someone who is concerned as I am with the same question. The monarchy is a true system because it is bound to an absolute center; to a being that belongs to humanity but not to the state. The king is a human being who has been called to a higher earthly destiny. This story necessarily urges itself on one. It alone satisfies a higher longing of our nature. Every person is to become worthy of the throne. The means of education for this distant goal is a king. Gradually he brings the mass of his subjects to resemble himself. Each has sprung from an ancient royal house. But how few still bear the stamp of this descent?

19.   It is a great mistake of our states that one sees the state too little. The state should be visible everywhere, every person should be identified as a citizen. Could not badges and uniforms be generally introduced? Whoever regards such things as trivial is not familiar with an essential quality of our nature.

20.   In times like the present a regent certainly cannot provide more appropriately for the preservation of his state than by seeking to individualize it to the greatest possible extent.

21.   The old hypothesis that comets were the revolutionary torches of the universe is assuredly valid for another kind of comet that periodically revolutionizes and rejuvenates the spiritual universe. The spiritual astronomer has long since noticed the influence of such a comet on a considerable part of the spiritual planet, which we call humanity. Mighty floods, changes in climate, irregularities of the center of gravity, a general tendency to deliquescence, strange meteors are the symptoms of this violent stimulus, whose consequence will determine the content of a new aeon. However necessary it may be that at certain periods everything should be brought to a state of flux in order to produce new, necessary mixtures and to cause a new, purer crystallization, it is none the less indispensable to alleviate this crisis and to prevent total deliquescence so that a stem remains, a kernel from which the new mass of crystals might grow and shape itself around it in new, beautiful forms. What is firm should gather itself together the more firmly so that excess phlogiston is lessened, and no effort should be spared to prevent the bones from softening and the characteristic fibers from dissolving.[10]
How nonsensical it would be to create a permanent crisis, and to believe the febrile state to be the true, healthy state, the preservation of which is all-important for the person. But otherwise, who could doubt its necessity, its beneficial effect.

22.   A time will come, and soon, when there will be a general conviction that no king could exist without a republic and no republic without a king, that the two are as indivisible as body and soul, and that a king without a republic and a republic without a king are only words without meaning. Hence a king always appeared at the same time as a true republic, and a republic appeared at the same time as a true king. The true king will be a republic, the true republic a king.

23.   Those who declaim in our time against princes as such and define salvation only in the new, French manner, who also recognize the republic only in the form of representation, and maintain with certainty that the republic exists only where there are constituent and electoral assemblies, *directoire* and councils, municipalities and liberty trees—these are wretched Philistines, empty of spirit and poor in heart, devotees of the letter who try to hide their shallowness and inner nakedness behind the bright banners of triumphant fashion, under the imposing mask of cosmopolitanism, and who deserve to have opponents like the obscurantists, so that the war of the frogs and mice might be perfectly reenacted.[11]

24.   Does not the king become the king simply through the inner conviction of *her* worth?[12]

25.   What was the first day for other princes will here be the lifetime of the king. The reign of most lasts only for the first day. The first day is the life of these ephemeral ones. Then they die, and their relics are misused in all kinds of ways. Thus most so-called reigns are interregnums; the princes are only the sacred red wax that sanctions the decrees.

26.   What are orders? Will-o'-the wisps, or shooting stars. The ribbon of an order ought to be a milky way, but usually it is only a rainbow, the setting of a storm. A letter from the queen, a picture of her; those would be orders, distinctions of the highest kind; distinctions which would inflame the bearer to perform the most distinguished deeds. Deserving housewives too should receive similar badges of honor.

27.   The queen, it is true, is not active on a large scale in political matters but rather in the domestic sphere. Principally it falls to her as of right to educate her sex, to exercise oversight over children in their early years and over moral order in the house, to care for the poor and sick of the house, especially those of her sex, to decorate the house in a tasteful way, to organize family festivals and arrange the life of the court. She should have her own chancellery, and her husband would be her prime minister with whom she would discuss everything. The education of her sex would include abolition of the obvious institutions of its corruption. Ought not the queen to shudder on entering a town to find that the deepest degradation of her sex is a public trade? The most severe punishments would not be too harsh for these real traffickers in souls. A murder is much less reprehensible. What is praised as the security intended by it is a strange toleration of brutality. As little as the government ought to intervene in private

matters, it ought to investigate most stringently every accusation, every public scandal, every report or complaint of a dishonored subject. Who has
more right to protect the wronged sex than the queen? She must blush for
any stay in a town which contains institutions that shelter and cultivate vice.
Her example, moreover, will achieve infinitely much. Happy marriages
will become ever more frequent and domesticity more than a fashion. At
the same time she will be a true model of feminine dress. Dress is
assuredly a very accurate ethometer.[13] Regrettably, in Berlin it has always
been at a very low level, often below zero. What good results could not be
achieved among young women and girls in Berlin by the company of the
queen? In itself it would already be a mark of honor and would necessarily
cause public opinion to be morally aware once more; and in the end,
public opinion after all is the most powerful means of restoring and establishing morality.

28.   The behavior of the state depends on public moral attitudes. The
only basis for true reform of the state is the ennobling of these attitudes.
The king and queen as such can and must be the principle of public attitudes. There is no longer any monarchy if the king and the intelligence of
the state are no longer identical. Hence the king of France had been
ousted from the throne long before the Revolution, and so it was with
most of the princes of Europe. It would be a very dangerous sign for the
new Prussian state if people were to be too dull for the beneficial influences of the king and queen, if indeed there were to be a lack of apprecia-
tion of this classic couple. That must become apparent shortly. If these
two people of genius have no effect then the complete dissolution of the
modern world is certain, and the heavenly vision is nothing but the flash
of an expiring lifeforce, the music of the spheres of a dying person, the visible premonition of a better world that awaits more noble generations.

29.   The court is actually the large-scale model of a household. The
great households of the state fashion themselves according to this, the
small ones imitate these and so on down the line. What a powerful effect
a court reform might have! The king is not to be frugal like a countryman
or a landed gentleman; but there is also such a thing as royal frugality, and
the king seems to be familiar with this. The court is to be classic private
life writ large. The housewife is the mainspring of domestic life. So too
the queen is the mainspring of the court. The man provides, the woman
orders and arranges. A frivolous household for the most part is the fault of
the woman. Everyone knows that the queen is entirely antifrivolous. That

is why I cannot comprehend how she can endure court life as it is. Her taste also, which is so intimately one with her heart, must find its colorless monotony unbearable.

Except for theater and concerts, and now and then interior decoration, one encounters almost no trace of good taste in the usual court life of Europe, and even those exceptions—how often are they tasteless or enjoyed in a tasteless way. But how extremely varied it could be. A gifted *maître des plaisirs*, guided by the taste of the queen, could make of the court an earthly paradise, he could follow the simple theme of the enjoyment of life through inexhaustible variations, and thus show us the objects of general veneration in ever new, ever charming surroundings. But what feeling is more heavenly than that of knowing that one's loved ones are engaged in the truest form of enjoyment of life.

30.   Every cultivated woman and every careful mother should have the queen's picture in her own or her daughters' living room. What a beautiful, strong reminder of the original image which each of us has set ourselves to reach. Similarity with the queen would become the character trait of the new Prussian women, their national trait. One gracious being among a thousand figures. At each wedding it would be easy to introduce a meaningful ceremony of tribute to the queen; and so with the king and queen one would be able to ennoble ordinary life, as the ancients once did with their gods. There true religious feeling arose through constantly blending the world of the gods with life. In the same way, here too true patriotism could arise through constantly weaving the royal couple into domestic and public life.

31.   Good society in Berlin should seek to procure the Schadow sculpture, set it up in the assembly room and found a lodge devoted to moral grace.[14] This lodge could be an educational institution for young women of the cultivated classes, and royal service would then be what the service of God is in a similar way, true distinction and reward of the most excellent of their sex.

32.   Formerly one had to flee from the courts with wife and children as from an infectious place. Now one will be able to withdraw from general moral degradation to a court as to a happy isle. Formerly a prudent young man had to go into the more remote provinces to find a worthy wife, or at least to families quite distant from town and court; in the future one will be able to go to court as to the gathering place of the best and most beauti-

ful, as it should be according to the original idea, and to count oneself fortunate to receive a wife from the hand of the queen.

33.   This king is the first king of Prussia. Every day he sets the crown on his own head, and no negotiations are necessary for him to be acknowledged.

34.   The king and queen protect the monarchy better than 200,000 soldiers.

35.   Nothing is more refreshing than talking about our desires when they are already being fulfilled.

36.   No state has been governed more like a factory than Prussia since the death of Frederick William I.[15] However necessary such mechanical administration perhaps may be for the physical health, strengthening, and proficiency of the state, in essence the state will perish if it is treated purely in this manner. The principle of the famous old system is to bind everyone to the state through self-interest. Clever politicians had the ideal of a state in front of them, where the interest of the state, selfish like the interest of the subjects, would yet be artificially bound to the latter in such a way that each would advance the cause of the other.

A great deal of effort has been expended on this political squaring of the circle: but raw self-interest seems to be totally imponderable, antisystematic. It has not proved possible to confine it at all, something which the nature of every state arrangement necessarily requires. Still this formal acceptance of common egoism as a principle has caused enormous harm, and the germ of the revolution of our time lies nowhere but here.

With growing civilization, needs had to become more diverse, and the value of the means of satisfying them had to rise all the more, the further moral attitudes had lagged behind all these luxurious inventions, all the refinements of the enjoyment of life and comfort. Sensuality had too quickly gained enormous ground. In just the same proportion as people cultivated this side of their nature, and became lost in the most multifarious activity and the most comfortable feeling of self, the other side had to seem to them insignificant, narrow and distant. Now they believed themselves to have taken the right path for their destiny and thought they had to apply all their forces to this. Thus coarse self-interest became a passion, and at the same time its basic principle emerged as the product of the highest understanding; it was this which made that passion so dangerous and invincible. How splendid it would be if the present king truly convinced himself that in this way one could only encounter the momentary good fortune of a gambler, which is determined by such a fickle quantity as the weakness of will and the lack of practice and finesse of the other players. Through being deceived one learns to deceive, how soon the card changes and the master becomes the pupil of his pupil. Only the just man and the just state can achieve lasting good fortune. What use to me are riches if they only stop at my house for fresh horses, the more quickly to complete their journey around the world? Selfless love in one's heart and its principle in one's head, that is the sole, eternal basis of all true, indissoluble bonds, and what else is the bond of state but a marriage?

37.   A king, like a father, must show no preference. He should not have only military companions and adjutants. Why not civilian ones as well? If in his military adjutants he trains capable generals for himself, why does he not want to train capable presidents and ministers in a similar way? He holds all the threads of government in his hands. Only from his perspective can all the machinery of state be observed. There alone one can learn to look at the state and its detail on a large scale. Nowhere can one be better trained for directorial posts than in the cabinet, where the political wisdom of the whole country is concentrated, where one receives each matter fully prepared, and from what place one can follow the course of affairs into its smallest tributaries. Here alone that circumscribed spirit will disappear, that pedantry of businessmen which allows them to place a singular value on their efforts and an infallible value on their suggestions, which makes them judge all things according to their own sphere of influence and vision, and often leads higher authorities themselves to one-sided, uneven, partial measures. This small-town character is visible everywhere, and is most responsible for hindering true republicanism, general participation in the whole state, close contact and harmony between all members of the state. The king ought to have still more military and civilian adjutants. As the former make up the highest military school in the state, so the latter would make up the highest practical and political academy in the state. A place in both would indeed be distinction and inspiration enough. For the king this varying company of the most admirable young men in the land would be highly agreeable and advantageous. But for these young men this apprenticeship would be the most resplendent celebration of their lives, the basis of lifelong enthusiasm. Personal love would join them forever to their sovereign, and the king would have the finest opportunity to come to know his servants

closely, to choose them and to respect and love them in person. The noble simplicity of the royal private life, the image of this happy pair, so closely bound to each other, would have the most beneficial influence on the moral education of this kernel of Prussian youth, and thus the king would most easily be guaranteed his inborn heart's desire, to become the true reformer and restorer of his nation and his age.

38.   Nothing ought to be more important to a king than to be and to remain as versatile, as informed, as well-oriented and free of prejudice, in short, as complete a person as possible. No human being has greater means at his disposal than a king to easily make this highest style of humanity his own. Through moving in society and continuing to learn he can keep himself forever young. An old king makes a state as morose as he is himself. How easy it would be for the king to become acquainted with the scientific progress of humanity. He already has learned academies. Now if he were to require of these complete, exact, and precise reports on the former and the present state of literature in general—regular reports on the most noteworthy events in everything that interests the human being as such—extracts from the most excellent books and notes on these, references to those products of fine art which deserved contemplation and enjoyment in their own right, and lastly suggestions for the further-ance of learned culture among his subjects, for the acceptance and sup-port of promising, important undertakings and of poor scholars of great promise, for filling scientific gaps and developing new literary seeds; or at least, if he established reciprocal relations, then this would put him in a position to view his state among other states, his nation within humanity and himself on a large scale, and here indeed to mold himself as a royal person. Spared the labor of an enormous amount of reading, he would enjoy the fruits of the learning of Europe in extract, and in a short time, through diligently reviewing this refined and concentrated material, he would be able to discern the breaking forth of new, mighty powers of his spirit, and to see himself in a purer element, at the height of his age. How divinatory his gaze would become, how astute his judgment, how sublime his temperament!

39.   A true prince is the artist of artists; that is, he is the director of artists. Every person should be an artist. Everything can become a fine art. Artists are the prince's material; his will is his chisel: he teaches, engages, and instructs the artists, because only he can oversee the picture as a whole from the right standpoint, because only to him the great idea, which is to

be represented and executed through combined forces and ideas, is perfectly present. The regent presents an infinitely diverse spectacle, where stage and parterre, actor and spectator are one, and he himself is poet, director, and hero of the play. How delightful if, as is so with the king, the *directrice* is at once the hero's beloved, the heroine of the play, if one sees in her even the muse who fills the poet with sacred fire, and tunes his instrument to play soft, heavenly melodies.

40.   In our time true miracles of transubstantiation have taken place. Does not a court transform itself into a family, a throne into a sanctuary, the royal nuptials into an eternal bond between two hearts?

41.   If the dove becomes the companion and darling of the eagle then the golden age is near or even already here, even if it is not yet publicly recognized and generally known.[16]

42.   Whoever wants to behold and come to love eternal peace now should travel to Berlin and see the queen. There everyone can convince himself with his own eyes that eternal peace loves heartfelt honesty above all things, and allows itself to be bound forever only by this.

43.   What should I wish for above all? I shall tell you: an inspired representation of the childhood and youth of the queen. Assuredly these years are in the truest sense a feminine apprenticeship. Perhaps nothing other than Natalie's apprenticeship. Natalie seems to me like the chance portrait of the queen.[17] Ideals must resemble each other.

44.   The reason for all error in attitudes and opinions is the confusion of the end with the means.[18]

45.   Most revolutionaries have not known exactly what they wanted — form or lack of form.

46.   Revolutions are evidence more against than for the real energy of a nation. There is a kind of energy stemming from sickliness and weakness — that has a more violent effect than the real kind — but which unfortunately ends in even more profound weakness.[19]

47.   If one passes judgment on a nation, one judges mostly that part of the nation that is primarily visible or striking.

48.   No argument is more disadvantageous to the ancien régime than that which one can draw from the disproportionate strength of members of the state, which manifests itself during a revolution. Its government

must have been highly flawed, given that many parts were able to become flawed and that such stubborn weakness took root everywhere.

49.   The weaker a part is the more it is inclined to disorder and inflammation.

50.   What are slaves? Completely weakened, repressed people. What are sultans? Slaves that have been excited by forcible stimuli. How do sultans and slaves end? Violently. The former easily as slaves, the latter easily as sultans, that is, delirious, frenzied. How can slaves be cured? Through freeing and enlightening them very cautiously. One must treat them like frozen people. Sultans? In the same way that Dionysius and Croesus were cured.[20] Beginning with terror, fasting, and confinement to a monastery and gradually rising to stimulants. Sultans and slaves are the extremes. There are still many middle grades up to the king and the true cynic — the grade of most perfect health. Terrorists and court lackeys belong more or less in the next grade to the sultans and slaves — and merge into each other as the latter do. Both represent the two forms of illness of a very weak constitution.

51.   The healthiest constitution with the maximum number of stimuli is represented by the king, the same with a minimum of stimuli — by the true cynic. The more equal the two are and the more they could exchange roles easily and without being fundamentally different, the more their constitution approaches the ideal of the perfect constitution. Thus the more independently of his throne the king lives the more he is king.

52.   All stimuli are relative — they are quantities — except for one which is absolute — and more than a quantity.

53.   The most perfect constitution arises through stimulation and absolute union with this stimulus. By means of this it can do without all others — for in the beginning it takes effect in proportion as the relative stimuli decline, and vice versa. But once the primary stimulus has entirely permeated the constitution the latter becomes entirely indifferent to the relative stimuli. This stimulus is — *absolute love.*

54.   A cynic and a king without love are so in name only.

55.   Every improvement of imperfect constitutions amounts to making them more capable of love.

56.   The best state consists of people of this kind who are neutral.

57.   In imperfect states these are also the best citizens. They take part in all good things, laugh privately at the petty tricks of their contemporaries, and keep well out of harm's way. They do not change because they know that every change of that kind and under these circumstances is only a new error, and the best cannot come from outside. They leave everyone their dignity, and just as they do not embarrass anyone—so also no one embarrasses them, and they are welcome everywhere.

58.   The present quarrel over forms of government is a quarrel over the relative advantage of mature age or blooming youth.

59.   The republic is the *fluidum deferens*[21] of youth. Where there are young people there is the republic.

60.   On marriage the system changes. The married man demands order, security, and calm—he wishes to live as a family, in one family—in a regulated household—he seeks a true monarchy.

61.   A prince lacking the spirit of the family is no monarch.

62.   But why be a single, limitless paterfamilias? To what caprice is one not then exposed?

63.   In all relative circumstances the individual is once and for all exposed to caprice—and if I went into the desert—is not my essential interest still exposed there to the caprice of my individuality? The individual, as such, is of his nature governed by *chance*. In a perfect democracy I am governed by very many, in representative democracy by fewer, in the monarchy by one capricious fate.

64.   But does not reason require that each of us is his own lawgiver? A person should only obey his own laws.

65.   If Solon and Lycurgus gave true, general laws, laws for humanity, from what source did they take these? It is to be hoped that they took them from the feeling of their humanity and their observation of it. If I am a human being as they were, from what source do I take my laws? Surely from the same one—and if I then live according to the laws of Solon and Lycurgus, am I indifferent to reason? Every true law is my law—let him pronounce and formulate it who will. But this pronouncement and formulation, or the observation of the original feeling and its representation, must not be so easy after all, otherwise would we have need of any spe-

cially written laws? Must it not therefore be an art? Thus also to apply the law seems indeed to presuppose lengthy practice and honing of the faculty of judgment. How did the estates and guilds arise? From lack of time and energy on the part of the individual. No person up to now was able to learn all the arts and sciences and to practice them at the same time—he could not be all in all to himself. The tasks and the arts were shared. Was that not also the case with the art of governing? According to the general demands of reason any person should be able to be a doctor, a poet, and so on. Moreover with the other arts it is for the most part already established that people are content not to be considered expert in them—except in the art of government and philosophy—for these, so everyone believes, one need only be possessed of audacity, and everyone is bold enough to speak about them like an expert and to aspire to practice them and to achieve virtuosity in them.

66.   But the excellence of representative democracy cannot be denied. A natural, exemplary person is a poet's dream. It follows that what remains—is the construction of an artificial one. The most excellent people in the nation complement each other—in this society a pure spirit of society bursts into flame. Its decrees are emanations of this spirit—and the ideal regent is realized.

67.   First I call into question the most excellent people in the nation and the ignition of pure spirit. I do not want even to make reference to very contradictory experience. It is obvious that a living body cannot be made out of dead materials—and that no just, unselfish, and liberal person can be put together out of unjust, selfish, and one-sided people. Indeed, that is precisely the error of a one-sided majority, and a long time will pass before people in general are convinced of this simple truth. A majority of this kind will not elect the most excellent, but on the average only the most narrow-minded and worldly-wise. The narrow-minded ones I take to be those for whom mediocrity has become second nature, the classical model of the herd. The worldly-wise ones—I take to be those who most cleverly pay court to the herd. Here no spirit will be ignited—least of all a pure one—one great mechanism will form—an inept routine—where only intrigue occasionally breaks through. The reins of government will swing to and fro between the letter of the law and the many faction-makers. The despotism of a single person has after all the advantage over this kind of despotism that the former plays with cards on the table, and at least then one saves time and shoe leather—if one has business with the

government—since in this case one does not always know at once in whose hands the government is to be found that day—and which ways are the most advantageous to choose to get there.

If the representative is to become more mature and refined—simply because of the height to which he is elevated, how much more will this be so with the single regent? If people were already what they should be and can become—then all forms of government would be the same—humanity everywhere would be ruled in the same way, and everywhere according to the original laws of humanity. But then one would choose at the outset the *most beautiful, most poetic*, the most natural form—the family form—monarchy. Several masters—several families, one master—one family!

68.   Now perfect democracy and the monarchy seem to be in a state of insoluble contradiction—the advantage of the one to be balanced by the opposite advantage of the other. Young people are on the side of the first, more sedate heads of households on the side of the second. This division seems to be caused by total divergence of inclination. One likes change—the other does not. Perhaps in certain years we all like revolutions, free competition, contests, and similar democratic phenomena. But for most people these years pass—and we feel attracted by a more peaceful world where a central sun leads the round dance, and one prefers to be a planet rather than join in a destructive struggle for the prelude to the dance. Thus let us at least be politically tolerant as we are in religious matters—let us at least accept the possibility that even a rational being could have different inclinations from ours. This tolerance, it seems to me, will gradually lead to the sublime conviction of the relativity of every positive form—and the true independence of a mature mind from every individual form, which is nothing to him but a necessary tool. The time must come when political entheism and pantheism will be most closely bound together as necessarily interchangeable parts.

6 *Teplitz Fragments*

1. Positive revision of the New Testament or the Christian religion.[1] Is not an embrace something similar to the Eucharist. More about the Eucharist.

2. Fundamental difference between the Old and the New Testaments. Why Palestine and the Jews were chosen for the foundation of the Christian religion. How the Jews were destroyed by it, like the French by the present Revolution. Medical view of the French Revolution—how did the French have to be cured—plan of their cure. How were we indirectly cured by means of it?
Asthenia of the Chinese—intervention of the Tartars. Medical treatment of the history of humanity.

3. Notes on daily life. On going to sleep—idleness—*eating*. Evening. Morning. The year—the week. Daily occupations and gatherings. Surroundings. Furniture. District, clothing etc.

4. Eating is only accentuated living. Eating—drinking—and breathing corresponds to the threefold division of the body into solid, liquid, and gaseous parts. The whole body breathes—only the lips eat and drink— they are just that organ which separates out again in manifold sounds what the spirit has prepared and the organ received through the other senses. The lips mean so much for sociability, how very much they deserve the kiss. Every gentle, soft elevation is a symbolic wish for touch. So everything in nature invites us figuratively and modestly to enjoy it—

and so the whole of nature might well be feminine, virgin and mother at the same time.

5.   Light is the symbol of true reflection. Thus by analogy light is—*the action*—of the *self-touching* of matter. The day is thus the consciousness of the planet, and while the sun like a god animates the center in perpetual autonomy, one planet after another closes one eye for a longer or shorter time and refreshes itself in cool sleep for new life and contemplation. Here too then there is religion—for is the life of the planets anything other than worship of the sun? Here too you come to meet us—ancient childlike religion of the Parsees—and we find in.you the religion of the universe.

6.   The *more the object*—the greater the love for it—an absolute object is met with absolute love. I come back to you, noble Kepler, whose lofty mind created for itself a spirit-filled, moral universe, rather than as in our times it is held to be wisdom—to kill everything, to bring down what is high instead of elevating what is low—and even to submit the spirit of humanity to the laws of mechanics.

7.   So what is *the sun*? A body that can only be set in motion by itself—and which consequently is an always autonomous, ever-luminous body. And a planet? A relatively movable body which is attuned to outside stimulus.

8.   Light is the vehicle of the community—of the universe. Does not true reflection play the same part in the spiritual sphere?

9.   Like ourselves, the stars float between illumination and darkening in turn—but even in the state of darkness we are granted, as they are, a consoling, hopeful glimmer of companion stars that are luminous and illuminated.

10.   Comets are truly eccentric beings—capable of the greatest illumination and the greatest darkening—a true *Dschinnistan*[2]—inhabited by powerful good and evil spirits—filled with organic bodies that can extend themselves as gas—and condense themselves as gold.

11.   Eating together is an activity that is symbolic of union. All kinds of union other than marriage are specifically directed activities, determined by an object and mutually determining this. On the other hand, marriage is an independent, total union. All partaking, appropriation and assimilation is eating, or rather eating is nothing but appropriation. Hence all spir-

itual partaking can be expressed by eating. In friendship one does indeed eat of one's friend, or lives by him. It is a true trope to substitute the body for the spirit—and with every commemorative meal of a friend, with bold, suprasensual imagination to partake of his flesh in each mouthful, and his blood in each draught. This certainly seems barbaric to the feeble taste of our times—but no one demands that they think straightaway of raw, corruptible flesh and blood. Corporeal appropriation is mysterious enough to be a beautiful image of spiritual *conviction*—and are flesh and blood really something so repulsive and ignoble? Truly there is more here than gold and diamonds, and the time is not far off when one will have higher ideas of the organic body.

Who knows what a sublime symbol is blood? Precisely the repulsive aspect of its organic components allows us to conclude that there is something very sublime in them. We shudder at them as we do at ghosts, and in this strange mixture we sense with childlike terror a mysterious world that might be an old acquaintance.

But to come back to the commemorative meal—might it not be possible to think that our friend was now a being whose flesh could be bread and whose blood could be wine?

In this way we partake of the genius of nature every day and thus every meal becomes a commemorative meal—a meal that nourishes the soul as it sustains the body—a mysterious means of transfiguration and deification on earth—of vivifying contact with that which is absolutely alive. We partake of the nameless one in sleep. We awaken like a child at its mother's breast and recognize how we received every element of refreshment and sustenance out of grace and love, and that air, food, and drink are components of an inexpressible, dear person.

12.   Only drinking glorifies poetry? What if poetry were also a liquid soul? Eating awakens wit and mood—that is why gourmands and fat people are so witty—and why joking and merry conversation comes so easily while eating. It also affects other solid abilities. At the table we are glad to engage in disputes and arguments, and there is much truth that is found at the table. Wit is spiritual electricity—solid bodies are necessary for that. Friendships too are easily created at the table—most easily among steely people—who does not sense the magnetism of souls here? Time at the table is the most remarkable period of the day—and perhaps the purpose—the blossom of the day. Breakfast is the bud. In this respect the ancients had a better insight into the philosophy of life—they ate only

once apart from breakfast—and that toward evening, after their business was over. Eating twice weakens interest. Between eating—theater, music and reading. The meal itself is a curve, as the true theory of education for life would have it. The lightest dish should be first—then heavier—then a very light dish again at the end. The meal should last a long time—through the period of digestion—in the end it is closed with sleep.

13.   The demand to accept the present world as the best and that which is absolutely mine is quite like the demand to accept my wedded wife as the *best* and only one, and to live wholly for her and in her. There are very many similar demands and claims—the recognition of which becomes a duty for a person who has resolved forever to respect everything *that has happened*—who is *historically religious*—the absolute believer and mystic of all history—the true *lover* of destiny. Fate is history made mystical. Every voluntary love in the accepted meaning is a religion—which has only one apostle, evangelist, and disciple—and can be a changing religion—but does not need to be.
Where the object of its nature excludes jealousy—then it is the Christian religion—Christian love.

14.   Nothing is more attainable for the spirit than the infinite.

15.   Sofie, or on women.[3]

16.   Might not the circumstance that the extremes of their formation are much more striking than ours speak for the superiority of women. The most depraved fellow is not so different from the most worthy man as the wretched hussy is from a noble woman. And is it not also that one finds very much good spoken of men but nothing good of women yet.

17.   Are they not similar to the infinite in that they cannot be squared, but can be found only through approaching them?[4] And similar to the highest in that they are absolutely close to us and yet always sought—that they are absolutely understandable and yet not understood, that they are absolutely indispensable and yet are mostly dispensed with, and similar to higher beings in that they appear so childlike, so ordinary, so idle, and so playful?

18.   Would we also love them if this were not the case. With women love came into being, and with love women—and therefore one cannot understand the one without the other. Anyone wanting to find women without love and love without women is like the philosophers who looked

at instinct without the object and the object without instinct—and did not see both at once in the concept of action.

19.   The beautiful secret of the virgin, precisely what makes her so inexpressibly attractive, is the premonition of motherhood—the sensing of a future world that slumbers within her and is to be developed from her. She is the most accurate image of the future.

20.   Charcoal and diamonds are one substance—and yet how different. Should it not be the same with man and woman. We are made of clay—and women are jewels and sapphires that also consist of clay.

21.   Philosophy of life comprises the study of the independent, *self-made* life, that which is within my power—and belongs to the theory of the art of life—or to the system of precepts on preparing such life for oneself.
Everything historical refers to a given—just as on the other hand everything philosophical refers to something *made*.
But history too has a *philosophical part.*

22.   Our opinion, belief, conviction of the difficulty, ease, permissibility and impermissibility, possibility and impossibility, success and lack of success etc. of an undertaking or an action indeed determines these—for example, it is somewhat laborious and harmful if I believe that this is so, and so on. Even the success of knowledge rests on the power of belief. In all knowledge there is belief.

23.   Even grammar is partly philological—the other part is philosophical.

24.   The secluded education of girls is so advantageous for domestic life and happiness because the man with whom they afterwards enter into the closest connection makes so much the deeper and more unique impression on them, which is indispensable for marriage. The first impression is the most powerful and most faithful, it always returns, even if it can seem to be erased for a period.

25.   The world is a *universal trope* of the spirit—a symbolic picture of it.

26.   That which is known, to which the philosopher must reduce everything and with which he must start, must be the originally known—the absolutely known. Everything perfect is natural to us and absolutely known.

27.   All enchantment is an artificially aroused madness.[5] All passion is enchantment—a charming girl is a more real enchantress than we think.

28.   Every book which a person has written intentionally or otherwise as himself—which is thus not only a book but the written thoughts and expressions of his character—can be judged in as many ways as the person himself. Here it is not an artist who is competent to make a judgment but a true connoisseur of men—it is appropriate not for an artistic forum but an anthropological one. However one-sided and unfair, however arbitrary and inhumane our judgment of people is—it is the same with works of this kind. There is so little *mature* sense of universal humanity—that one cannot be surprised at the criticisms of these works. It is precisely the best of them which is most easily overlooked. Here too the connoisseur, for whom a person is not really present unless he has seen him with his own eyes, finds countless nuances, harmonies, and felicities—only he knows how to appreciate, and perhaps he admires in a very mediocre or even bad-seeming work a rare combination and development of human talents—the splendid natural art of a spirit which reveals itself to him in a barbaric form only because it did not possess the talent of written expression or neglected it.

29.   Brown is the physician of our age. The reigning constitution is the sickly one—the asthenic. The system of healing is the natural product of the reigning constitution—hence it must change with the latter.

30.   Only he who has no need of society is *bon compagnon*. Only such a one becomes independent of society. He can possess it and attract it in many ways and plan to treat it as he will. Others are possessed by him—and do not possess him. Society does not need to attract me if I wish to attract it. It must have appetite for me and I must be able to adapt myself to its constitution, a talent which in general could be called *tact*. I must only have the *passive will* to yield, to allow myself to be enjoyed, to communicate myself.

31.   *Les Femmes* are models of the sickliest, most feminine constitution—*the highest asthenias*—with a minimum of reason.[6] In this way they become very comprehensible. They are annihilators of reason.
On *fashion*. Ought the highest attraction for an asthenic man to be an asthenic woman? and conversely.

32.   Might there perhaps be a lady who would dress well from genuine love of ornament—from unselfish taste?

33.   An empiricist is: one whose way of thinking is an effect of the external world and of fate—the passive thinker—to whom his philosophy is given. Voltaire is a pure empiricist and so are several French philosophers—Ligne tends imperceptibly to the transcendent empiricists.[7] These make the transition to the dogmatists. From there the way leads to the enthusiasts—or the transcendent dogmatists—then to Kant—then to Fichte—and finally to magical idealism.[8]

34.   The *history of the philosophers* belongs to philological philosophy. Up to now the history of the education of humanity, the history of the philosophers, and history of philosophy have always been confused— only *lexicographical* completeness has been sought—and as a result just those hermaphrodites—and monsters—come into being, so that for example under the article "Philosophy" everything is brought together which even touches on philosophy in any way, anywhere the word philosophy etc. can be found.[9]

35.   Of how few peoples is a history possible! A people earns this superiority only by a literature or works of art, for otherwise what part of it endures that is individual or characteristic. It is natural that a people does not become historical until it becomes a public. Is a person then historical—before he attains his *majority* and counts as his own being?

36.   The heart is the key to the world and to life. One lives in this helpless condition in order to love—and to be beholden to others. Through imperfection one becomes open to the influence of *others*—and this influence of others is the purpose. In *illnesses* only *others ought* and *can* help us. Thus Christ, from this *point of view*, is indeed the *key to the world.*

37.   *Economics* in the broadest sense also embraces the theory of the order of life. It is the *practical* science as a whole. Everything practical is economic.

38.   Sensation of the self—like thinking of the self—active sensation. One brings the organ of sensation into one's power like the organ of thought.

39.   *Hypochondria* paves the way for *physical* self-knowledge—self-mastery—*self-living.*[10]

40.   Ordinary life is a priestly service—almost like that of the vestals. We are occupied with nothing other than the preservation of a sacred and mysterious flame—a double one, it appears. It depends on us how we

look after it and attend it. Might the style of its care perhaps be the yard-stick of our loyalty, love, and care for the highest—the character of our being? Loyalty to our calling? Symbolic sign of our religious feeling—that is, of our being? (fireworshipers)

41.   Our *whole life is divine service*.

42.   Most writers are at once their own *readers*—as they write—and that is why so many traces of the reader appear in their works—so many critical considerations—so much which is the province of the reader and not the writer. Dashes—words in capitals—emphasized passages—all this belongs to the sphere of the reader. The reader places the *accent* at will—he really makes of a book what he will. Is not every reader a philologist? There is no *generally valid reading*, in the usual sense. Reading is a free operation. No one can prescribe to me how and what I am to read.
Is not the writer to be at the same time a philologist raised to the power of infinity—or not a philologist at all? The last possesses *literary innocence*.

43.   An idea is the more solid and *individual*—and stimulating—the more diverse thoughts, worlds, and moods *converge* and touch each other in it.
If a work has several *causes*, several meanings, multiple interest, in general several aspects—several ways of being understood and loved, then it is assuredly extremely interesting—a genuine outflow of the *personality*. Just as the most elevated and the most common people resemble each other to a certain extent, as do those who are comprehensible at the most elevated and the most common level—so it is also with books. Perhaps the *most elevated book* resembles an ABC book. In general, what is true of human beings is true of those books and all others. The human being is a source of analogy for the universe.

44.   The innocence of the king and queen. The beginning of government. The demands on him. Does a king need to have very many cares? Prussia's *prospects*. Finances. On my essay. *The king's imagination*.[11]

45.   The postulate of feminine mysticism is entrenched. Unconditional love of the best available object is everywhere demanded of women. What a high opinion of the free force and self-creative power of their spirit this presupposes.

46.   The *play of the eyes* allows a great range of expression. The other gestures of the face, or *expressions*, are only the consonants to the vowels

of the eyes. Thus physiognomy is the language of gesture of the face. When we say a person has a lot of physiognomy it means—his face is a *complete, accurate,* and *idealizing* speech organ. Women have a supremely idealizing physiognomy. They can express *sensations* not only truthfully but also attractively and with beauty, ideally. Extended association with them teaches one to understand the language of the face. The most perfect physiognomy must be *generally and absolutely comprehensible.* The eyes could be called a *light keyboard.*[12] The eye expresses itself by higher and lower sounds in a similar way to the throat, the vowels by weaker and stronger gradations of light. Might not colors be the light consonants?

47.   *Moods—indeterminate sensations,* not definite sensations and feelings, make for happiness. One will feel well when one notices no particular impulse—no definite thoughts or series of sensations within oneself. Like light, this condition is also only brighter or darker. *Specific thoughts* and *sensations are its consonants.* It is called consciousness. It can be said of the most perfect consciousness that it is conscious of all and nothing. It is *song*—merely modulation of *moods*—as song modulates the vowels— or sounds. The inner *self-language* can be dark, heavy, and barbaric—or Greek and Italian—it is the more perfect the more it approaches song. The expression "He does not understand himself" appears here in a new light. *Formation of the language of consciousness.* Perfection of the expression. *Skill of carrying on a conversation with oneself.* Our thinking is therefore a *dialogue*—our feeling—sympathy.

48.   The *greatest magician* would be he who could also enchant himself, in such a way that his enchantments would appear to him like autonomous phenomena created by others. Might that not be the case with us.

49.   Strangely enough, seasons, days, life, and destinies are all entirely *rhythmical*—metrical—accented. In all arts and *crafts,* all *machines*—in organic bodies, our daily tasks—everywhere—rhythm—meter—beat— melody. Everything we do with a certain skill—we do rhythmically without noticing it. Rhythm occurs everywhere—creeps in everywhere. All mechanism is *metrical*—rhythmical. There must be more behind this— might it be merely the influence of inertia?

50.   Mechanical divine service. The Catholic religion is far more *visible—more integrated* and more familial than the Protestant. Apart from

the church spires and the clerical *dress*—which is after all very modified—one sees nothing of the latter.

51.   Women—children. Style of *conversation* with them. The models of
ordinary femininity feel the boundaries of existence in each case very precisely—and *conscientiously* guard against overstepping them. Hence *their*
famed *ordinariness—practical people of the world*. They themselves dis-
like exaggerated subtleties, delicacies, truths, virtues, inclinations. They
like variation of the commonplace—novelty of the ordinary—no new
ideas, but new clothes—uniformity in the whole—superficial attractions.
They love dancing principally because of its *lightness*, vanity, and sensuality. Wit that is too good is fatal to them—just as is everything beautiful,
great, and noble. Mediocre and even bad reading, actors, plays etc.—that
is for them.

52.   Absolute hypochondria. Hypochondria must become an *art*—or a
kind of training.

7   *On Goethe*

1.   Goethe is a wholly practical poet.[1] He is in his works—what the Englishman is in his goods—extremely simple, neat, comfortable, and durable. He has done for German literature what Wedgwood has for the English art world. Like the Englishman he has a naturally economical and noble taste acquired through the understanding. Both qualities tolerate each other very well and have a close affinity, in the *chemical* sense. In his scientific studies it becomes very clear that his inclination is rather to finish completely something insignificant—to give it the greatest polish and ease of expression, than to begin a whole world and do something in respect of which one can know in advance that it will not be possible to carry it out completely, that it will probably remain clumsy and that a masterly level of skill will never be achieved in it. In this field too he chooses a Romantic or otherwise nicely convoluted subject. His observations on light, on the transformation of plants and insects are at once confirmations and the most convincing proofs that the perfect didactic essay also belongs to the realm of the artist.[2] One would also be justified in maintaining in a certain sense that Goethe is the first physicist of his age—indeed that his work is epoch-making in the history of physics. There can be no question of the scope of his knowledge, however little any discoveries may determine the rank of the scientist. It is a question of whether one contemplates nature as an artist does antiquity—for nature is nothing other than living antiquity. Nature and insight into nature come into being at the same time, like antiquity and the knowledge of antiquities; for one is greatly in error if one believes that antiquities exist. Antiquity is only now coming into being. It grows under the eyes and soul

111

of the artist. The remains of ancient times are only the specific stimuli for the formation of antiquity. Antiquity is not made with hands. The spirit produces it through the eye—and the carved stone is only the body which first receives meaning through antiquity and becomes its appearance.[3] As Goethe the physicist is to other physicists, so Goethe the poet is to other poets. Here and there he is surpassed in range, diversity, and profundity, but in the art of creation, who could aspire to be his equal? With him everything is deed—as with others everything is only tendency. He really makes something, while others only make something possible—or necessary. We are all necessary and possible creators—but how few of us are real ones. The scholastic philosopher would perhaps call this active empiricism. We shall content ourselves with contemplating Goethe's artistic talent and casting another glance at his understanding. By this one can come to see the gift of generalization in a new light. He generalizes with a rare exactitude, but never without at the same time representing the object to which the generalization corresponds. This is nothing but applied philosophy—and so in the end we should find him, with more than a little astonishment, to be also a practical philosopher who applies his knowledge, as every true artist after all has always been. Even the *pure* philosopher will be practical, although the applied philosopher does not need to engage in pure philosophy—for this is an art in itself. Goethe's *Meister.* The seat of authentic art is solely in the understanding. The latter construed according to a particular concept. Imagination, wit, and judgment are required only by this. Thus *Wilhelm Meister* is entirely an art product—a work of the understanding. From this point of view one sees many very mediocre works in the art gallery—on the other hand most works of literature that are considered excellent are excluded. The Italians and the Spanish show talent for art far more frequently than we do—the English have much less and are similar in this respect to ourselves, who also possess *talent for art* extremely rarely—even if among all nations we are best and most richly provided with those abilities—which the understanding employs in its works. This excess of the requisite qualities for art certainly makes the few artists among us so unique—so outstanding, and we can be sure that the most splendid works of art will be produced among us, for no nation can surpass us in energetic universality. If I understand the most recent admirers of the literature of antiquity correctly, they have with their demand that we imitate the classical writers no other purpose than to cultivate artists for us—to awaken the talent for art in us. No modern nation has possessed the understanding of art in

such high degree as the ancients. Everything for them is a work of art —
but perhaps it would not be saying too much to assume that it is only for
us that they are or can be so. Classical literature is like antiquity; it is not
really given to us — it is not present — rather it is to be only now produced
by us.[4] Through diligent and inspired study of the ancients, classical literature is only now coming into being for us — a literature that the ancients
themselves did not have. The ancients would have had to apply themselves to the contrary task — for he who is only an artist is a one-sided, narrow person. Goethe may well not be the equal of the ancients in
rigor — but he surpasses them in content — which merit however is not his
own. His *Meister* approaches them closely enough — for how very much is
it an absolute novel, without any adjective — and how much that is in our
time!

Goethe will and must be surpassed — but only as the ancients can be surpassed, in content and energy, in diversity and profundity — not really as
an artist — or only by very little, for his rightness and his rigor are perhaps
already more exemplary than they appear.

2.   Consummate philosophers arrive easily at the principle — that philosophy too is vain — and so too in all branches of learning.

3.   A prime minister, a prince, a director of any kind only needs *people*
and *artists — knowledge* of character and talent.

4.   World psychology. It will not be possible to explain the organism
without presupposing a *world soul*, nor the world plan without presupposing a world rational being.

If in explaining the organism no attention is paid to the *soul* and to the
mysterious bond between *it and the body*, not much progress will be
made. Perhaps life is nothing other than the result of this union — the
action of this contact.

As light results from the friction of steel against stone, sound from touching the bow and the string, vibration from closing and opening the galvanic chain, so perhaps life results from the awakening (penetration) of
organic matter.

Indirect construction. Right appears of itself if the conditions for its appearance occur. A *mechanical operation* relates entirely to the higher *result* as
steel, stone, and contact relate to the spark. *Free joint action.*

Every action is accompanied by a higher genius.

The individual soul should be in agreement with the world soul. Mastery
of the world soul and joint mastery of the individual soul.

5.   On the diverse ways *to have effect* or to *stimulate*—(through intervention, thrust, contact, immediate contact, *pure existence, possible existence*, etc.)

6.   *Dramatic* kind of story telling. Fairy tales and *Meister*. *Toujours en état de Poësie*.

7.   High value of mathematics as *active* science. Preeminent interest of *mechanics*. (Study of contact. Acoustics). Various kinds of contacts—and tangents. Active and passive tangents. Angle of contacts. Speed of the contacts or beats. Series or sequences of beats. Line beats. Point beats. Surface beats. Mass beats. *Persistent beats*.

8.   Foundations of geology and mineralogy. Critique of the *criteria*.[5]

9.   Theory of instruments—or *organology*.

10.   Light is certainly action—light is like life, *effective effect*—something which *reveals* itself only on the conjunction of appropriate conditions. Light makes fire. Light is the *genius* of the fire process.
Life, like *light*, is capable of intensification and weakening and gradual *negation*. Does it also break up into *colors* as light does? The process of nutrition is not the cause but only the *result* of life.

11.   All effect is *transition*. In chemistry both of these merge into the other and change it. That is not the case with what is called mechanical influence.

12.   Characteristic of *illness*—the instinct for self-destruction. So it is with everything imperfect—so it is even with life—or better, with organic matter.
Dissolution of the difference between life and death. Annihilation of death.

13.   Ought not all changes which bodies mutually produce in each other to be merely changes in capacity and excitability, and all chemical operations and influences to be *generally uniform* in that they modify the excitability and capacity of every kind of matter. Thus, for example, oxygen has this effect in the combustion process. All chemical elements are indirectly in accord. The characteristics and appearances of each substance depend on its *excitability*. All changes in compounds refer to the capacity and excitability of the bodies. Bodies differ as a result of their diverse excitability.

Or could it be said that bodies would most naturally be classified as a result of their diverse relations to *excitability*, as *stimuli*?

All this fits very well with galvanism. Chemistry is already galvanism — galvanism of inorganic nature. Fire is merely an *aid* — a learned means for the chemist.

Spontaneous combustion is galvanization. The calces of metals have not yet been used enough in medicine.

Does heat have a chemical effect? Not in the stricter sense — it only furthers galvanizations.

14.   Cold is an *indirect stimulus* — in healthy bodies it entices more warmth to be produced. Nothing keeps a quite healthy person in a state of lively activity as much as alternating deficiency and excess of stimuli. The *deficiency stimulates* him to replace it — the excess causes him to moderate and confine the function, excess determines him to diminish *activity*. *Deficiency* brings about *activity* in the healthy person — excess brings out *rest*. Might works of art not be products of healthy inactivity?

15.   The instinct for organization is the instinct to transform everything into tool and means.

16.   Journals are really *communal* books. Writing in a social group is an interesting symptom — which hints at a further great development of the writing business. Perhaps sometime people will write, think, and act en masse — whole communities, even nations will undertake a work.

17.   Every person who consists of *persons* is a person to the second power — or a *genius*. In this respect one may well say that there were no Greeks but only a Greek genius. An educated Greek was his own work only in a very mediated way and to a very slight extent. This explains the great and pure individuality of Greek art and science, while it cannot be denied that on some *flanks* Egyptian and oriental mysticism attacked and modernized it. In *Ionia* the softening influence of the warm Asiatic sky could be noticed, just as on the other hand in the earliest Dorian mass one became aware of the mysterious reserve and severity of the Egyptian gods. Later writers have often taken up this old style as a result of the Romantic and modern instinct; they have animated these crude figures with a new spirit, placing them among their contemporaries, in order to bring them to a halt in the facile progress of civilization and turn their attention back to the sacred objects that have been abandoned.

18.   In earlier times only *nations* lived—or geniuses. Genius to the second power. Hence, the ancients must be regarded en masse.

19.   The question of the *reason*, the law of a phenomenon etc. is an abstract one, that is, it is a question directed away from the object toward the spirit. It has to do with *appropriation*, assimilation of the object. Through explanation the object ceases to be strange.
The spirit strives to absorb the stimulus. What is strange stimulates it. Transformation of what is *strange* into one's own; thus, appropriation is the ceaseless business of the spirit. One day there is to be no *stimulus* and nothing *strange* any more—the spirit is to be strange and stimulating to itself, or will be able to make it so intentionally. Now the spirit is spirit out of instinct—a nature spirit. It is to be a rational spirit, to be spirit out of reflection and *art*.
Nature is to become art and art is to become second nature.

20.   The matter of dispute between pathologists of the humors and the nerves is a matter of dispute in common among the physicists. This dispute touches on the highest problems of *physics*.
The pathologists of the humors correspond to those who seek to multiply matter—the prophets of matter. The pathologists of the nerves correspond to the atomistic, mechanical prophets of form. True *actionists*, like Fichte etc., unite both systems. One can call these last creative *observers*, *creators of seeing*. These two are those who are directly and indirectly inert—liquid and solid ones.
The concept of action can be divided into the concepts of *matter* and *movement* (thrust). Thus the actionist divides into the *humoralists* and the *neurotomists*. They are its closer elements—its *nearest* components.[6]

21.   Similarity of historical geology and mineralogy to philology.

22.   Sciences divide into sciences—meanings into meanings. The more limited and determined, the more practical. On the tendency of scholars to universalize their science. Diverse objects become one object because of the fact that different meanings become one.

23.   Representation of an object in *series*—(series of variations—*modifications* etc.). Such for example is the representation of the characters in *Meister*. In self-reflection—in things at first-, second-, third-hand, etc. Such is for example a historical series, a collection of engravings from the crudest beginning of the art until its perfection and so on—of the forms from the frog to Apollo etc.

24.   Poetry is the truly absolute real. This is the heart of my philosophy. The more poetic the more true.

25.   On the sensations of *thinking* in the *body*.[7]

26.   *Antiquities*.[8] The Madonna. The human being is a self-given historical individual. Gradual humanity. If humanity has reached the highest stage, then the higher one will reveal itself and continue of itself. View of the history of humanity—the mob—the nations—societies—individual people. Elevation of mechanics. Fichte's intellectual chemistry. Chemistry is *passionate ground*. Chemistry is the crudest and earliest formation. *Descriptions of paintings* etc. On *landscape painting*—and in general painting as against sculpture. Everything must be able to be squared and not squared at the same time.[9] Utilization, use is infinitely gradual—so too measurement. Landscapes—*surfaces—structures—architectonic structures*. Cave *landscapes*. Atmospheres, cloud landscapes. The whole landscape is to form one individual—vegetation and inorganic nature—liquid, solid nature—*male—female*. Geological landscapes. Nature variations. Must not sculpture and painting be symbolic. The art gallery is a storeroom of indirect stimuli of all kinds for the poet. *Necessity* of all works of art. Every work of art has an ideal a priori—it has a necessity of itself to *exist*. Only through this does a true critique of painters become possible. Suite of madonnas. Suite of heroes. Suite of wise men. Suite of geniuses. Suite of gods. Suite of human beings.[10]
One is compelled by the antiquities to treat them as sacred objects.
Particular kinds of *souls* and *spirits*. Which live in trees, landscapes, stones, paintings. One must look at a landscape as one looks at a dryad and an oread. One should feel a landscape as one does a body. Every landscape is an ideal body for a particular *kind of spirit*. The sonnet. *Wit*. Sense of the *ancient world*—awakened by the antiquities.

27.   The poet borrows all his materials other than *images*.

28.   Perpetual virgins—born women. Fichte's apotheosis of Kantian philosophy. *Thinking* about thinking indeed teaches us to gain power over our thinking—because we learn thereby to think how and what we will. Inner, immensely wide, infinite universe—analogy with the external world—light—gravity.

29.   Must then all people be people, beings quite other than people can exist in human form. That educators should be virtuous is the indirectly positive principle of the art of education. *Universal skill of writing*. On

those who think many things—and those who think one thing—for example, Friedrich Schlegel and Fichte.

Trivialization of the divine and apotheosis of the commonplace. We have emerged from the period of generally valid forms. Influence of the material of sculpture on the figure—and its *effect*. Should the more attractive and the stronger effect of *finer* and *rarer* materials not be *galvanic*? *Compulsion* is a stimulus for the spirit—compulsion has something absolutely stimulating for the spirit. Medical application of happiness and unhappiness. On neutralization—complicated illnesses—local complaints—systems of procreation. All doubt, all need for *truth*—dissolution. Knowledge is the result of *rawness* and *overdevelopment*—a symptom of an imperfect constitution. All scientific *education* therefore tends toward making one clever—practice. All scientific *healing* tends toward *restitution* of health, where one has no scientific needs.

30.   All that is visible clings to the invisible. That which can be heard to that which cannot—that which can be felt to that which cannot. Perhaps the thinkable to the unthinkable.

The telescope is an *artificial, invisible organ. Vessel.*

The imagination is the marvelous sense that can *replace* all senses for us—and which already is so much directed by our will. If the external senses seem to be entirely governed by mechanical laws—then the imagination is obviously not bound to the present and to contact with external stimuli.

31.   The unity of the image, the form, of picturesque compositions rests on fixed relations, like the unity of musical harmony. Harmony and melody.

32.   Our body is a *part* of the *world*—or better, a limb: It already expresses the *independence*, the analogy with the whole—in short, the concept of the microcosm. This limb must correspond to the whole. As many senses, as many modes of the universe—the universe is a complete analogue of the human being in body, mind, and spirit. The latter is the abbreviation, the former the elongation of the same substance.

In general, I neither ought nor want to act at will on the world—for that purpose I have the body. Through modification of my body I modify *my* world for myself. Through not acting on the *vessel of my existence* I likewise shape my world indirectly.

33.   The tree can become for me a blossoming flame—the human being a speaking one—the animal a walking flame.[11]

34.   Everything that is perceived is perceived in proportion to its power of repulsion.
Explanation of the *visible* and the *illuminated*—on the analogy of perceptible heat. So also with sounds. Perhaps too with thoughts.

8 *General Draft*

1. PSYCHOLOGY AND ENCYCLOPEDISTICS.[1] Only through representation does anything become *clear*. One understands a thing most easily if one sees it represented. In this way one understands the self only in so far as it is represented by the nonself. The nonself is the symbol of the self, and serves only for the self-understanding of the self. Conversely, one understands the nonself only in so far as it is represented by the self and as this becomes its symbol. In respect of mathematics this observation can be applied thus: in order to be comprehensible, mathematics must be represented. One science can only be truly represented by another. The pedagogical foundations of mathematics must therefore be *symbolic* and *analogical*. A familiar science must serve as a simile for mathematics, and this basic comparison must become the principle of the representation of mathematics. Just as anthropology is the basis of human history so the physics of mathematics is the basis of the history of mathematics. Physics altogether is the original, actual history. What is usually called history is only derived history.

God himself can only be understood through representation.

PHILOSOPHY. Originally *knowledge* and *action* are *mixed*—then they separate and in the end they are to be *united* again, cooperating, harmonious, but not *mixed*.

We want *at once* to know and act in a mutual relationship—to know how and what we are doing, to do how and what we know.

Chemistry is the art of matter—unison, mechanics the art of movement—dissonance. *Physics*—synthesis. Chemistry and mechanics together (harmony) the art of life.[2]

121

2.   ENCYCLOPEDISTICS. Transcendental physics is the *first*, but the *lowest* science—like the *Theory of Scientific Knowledge*. It deals with *nature* before it *becomes nature*—in that condition where *mixture* and *movement* (matter and energy) are still one. Its subject is *chaos*. Transformation of chaos into harmonious *heaven* and *earth*. Concept of heaven. Theory of *true heaven*—the inner universe. Heaven is the *soul* of the astral system—and the latter is its body.

The modern view of the *appearances of nature* was either chemical or mechanical. The scholar of practical physics considers nature as at once *independent* and *self-modifying*, and as *harmoniously at one* with the spirit. His chemistry is higher—it combines materials without destroying their individuality, and produces higher republican bodies. So too is his mechanics. The former shares with the latter one medium, matter and movement *paired through mutual inclination*—plus and minus, male and female form. Energy and matter in harmony—various materials and movements combine simultaneously. *Each one intends* itself *indirectly*. Moralization of nature.

Magical chemistry, mechanics, and physics belong in quite a different field.

Facture is opposed to *nature*. The spirit is the artist. Facture and nature mixed—separated—united. When they are mixed they deal with transcendental physics and poetics—when separated with practical physics and poetics—when united with higher physics and poetics.

The higher *philosophy* deals with the *marriage of nature and spirit*.

Chemical and mechanical psychology. Transcendental *poetics*. Practical poetics. Nature produces, the spirit makes.

PSYCHOLOGY. Love is the final purpose of *world history*—the *unum* of the universe.

3.   ARCHAEOLOGY. Galvanism of the antiquities, their *substance*—revivification of the ancient world.

Marvelous *religion*, which hovers around them—their history—the philosophy of sculpture—gems—human petrifactions—painting—portrait—landscapes. Man has always expressed the symbolic philosophy of his being in his works and his action and inaction. He announces himself and his gospel of nature. He is the messiah of nature. The antiquities are at once *products of the future and of times past*. Goethe contemplates nature like an antiquity—character of antiquity—the antiquities are from another world. They are as if fallen from heaven. The contemplation of the antiquities must be *taught* (physically) and *poetic*. Is there a central antiquity — or a universal spirit of the antiquities? Mystical sense of forms. The antiquities do not touch one but all senses, the whole human essence.

4.   COSMOLOGY. Henceforth one must separate God and nature — God has nothing to do with nature. He is the goal of nature — that with which it must one day be in harmony. Nature is to become *moral*, and so indeed the Kantian moral god and morality itself appears in quite a new light. The moral god is something far higher than the magical god.

5.   EDUCATION OF NATURE. Nature is to become moral. We are its *teachers* — its moral *tangents* — its moral stimuli.
Can morality, like the understanding etc., be objectified and *organized*. *Visible morality*.

6.   THEORY OF EDUCATION. It is assumed that the *child* (subject) has belief — the absolute *acceptance* of *a principle that awakens activity* (object).
PHILOSOPHY. *The beginning of the self* is merely *ideal*. If it had begun, then it must have begun in this way. The beginning is already a later concept. The beginning arises later than the self, therefore the self cannot have begun.[3] We see from this that here we are in the realm of *art*. But this artificial supposition is the basis of a genuine science which always derives from *artificial acts*. The self is to be constructed. The philosopher approaches this construction by creating artificial elements. This process is not the *natural history* of the self. Self is not a product of nature — it is not nature — not a historical being — but an artistic one — an *art* — a work of art. The natural history of man is the *other half*. The *theory of the self* and the *history of mankind* — or nature and art — are united in a higher *science* — (*moral theory of education*) — and *mutually perfected*. Through morality nature and art each arm the other into the infinite.

7.   THEORY OF HUMANITY. *A child is love that has become visible*. We ourselves are a seed of *love* that has become visible between nature and spirit or art.
THEOSOPHY. God *is love*. Love is the highest *reality* — the primary cause.
THEORY OF THE FUTURE. This *legal situation* must become a *moral* one — and then all barriers and conditions will fall away by themselves — and each is and has everything unharmed by the others. Mathematics refers only to *law* — legal nature and art — not *magical* nature and *art*. Both

become magical through *moralization*. *Love* is the foundation of the possibility of magic. Love works magically.
All *being* is to be transformed into a *having*. *Being* is *one-sided—having* is synthetic, *liberal*.

8.   ROMANTICISM. Making absolute—making universal. *Classification* of the individual moment, of the individual situation etc. is the authentic essence of *making Romantic*. See *Meister*. Fairy tale.[4]

9.   THEORY OF HISTORY. On the present moment—or the way earthly time is perpetually becoming torpid—it has a strange life flame. Time also *makes* everything, even if it *destroys*—binds—separates.
Nature of *memory—soul flame*—especial life of the soul—inner way of life—the process of becoming torpid.
This stems from touching a second world—a second life—where everything is reversed.
Like an electric spark, we leap across into the other world etc. Increase in capacity. Death is transformation—*repression of the individual principle*—which now enters into a new *more tenable, more capable* connection.

10.   THEORY OF NATURE. The more energetically that which is to be eaten resists, the livelier will the flame of the moment of enjoyment be. Application to oxygen. Rape is the most intense kind of enjoyment. Woman is our oxygen.[5]
THEORY OF NATURE. All kinds of excrement may well be fertilizing agents, for example, *dung*. Difference between the dung of animals and plants. Human seeds also flourish more quickly and luxuriantly if they are fertilized by *higher* dung.
As we fertilize the earth for the plants, so the plants fertilize the air for us. Plants are children of the earth—we are children of the ether (earth for solid bodies—ether for liquid ones). The lung is actually our rootlet. We are alive when we breathe and we begin our life with breathing.
We eat the plants and they flourish in our decay. What eating is to us, fructifying is to plants. *Conceiving* is female enjoyment—as consuming is for the male. A drunkard can be compared with a sluttish woman. Impregnation is the result of eating—it is the reverse operation. *Giving birth*, conceiving, is the opposite of impregnating, like eating. Man is to a certain extent also woman, as woman is man—Is this perhaps the origin of various kinds of modesty?

11. PHYSICS. The life of plants is maintained against the life of animals—an unceasing conceiving and giving birth—and the latter against the former—an unceasing eating and fructifying.

As *woman* is the *highest visible* food which makes the *transition from body to soul*—so also the sexual organs are the highest, *external* organs which make the transition from visible to invisible organs.

Looking—(speaking)—*touching of hands*—*kissing*—*touching the breast*—*grasping the sexual organs*—the act of embracing—these are steps on the ladder—on which the soul climbs down. Opposed to this is a ladder—on which the body climbs up—to the embrace. *Sensing*—*sniffing*—*the sexual act.* Preparation of the soul and the body to awaken the sexual drive.

Soul and body *touch* in the sexual act—*chemically*—or galvanically—or electrically—or *like fire.* The soul eats the body (and digests it?) *instantaneously*—the body conceives the soul (and gives birth to it?) instantaneously.

12. MAGIC. (mystical theory of language)
Sympathy of the *sign* with the signified. One of the basic ideas of cabbalism.[6]

Magic is quite different from philosophy etc. and forms a *world*—a branch of learning—an *art* of its own.

Magical astronomy, grammar, philosophy, religion, chemistry etc.

Theory of the *mutual representation of the universe.* Theory of emanation. (Personified emanations).

13. POLITICS. The perfect citizen lives entirely in the state—he has no property outside the state. International law is the beginning of universal legislation for the universal state. On alliances—peace agreements—treaties—*unions*—*guarantees.*

Republic and *monarchy* are perfectly united *through* an act of union. There must be several necessary levels of states—but they must be brought together through a *union.* JURISPRUDENCE. Otherwise Roman law has been regarded as specifically Roman, and so with much else. The trial *is the process of generating judgment*—of law—something like a proof. The general trial.

14. ROMANTICISM et cetera. In a true fairy tale everything must be marvelous—mysterious and unconnected—everything must be animated.[7] Each in its different way. The whole of nature must be mixed in a strange way with the whole of the spirit world. Time of general anarchy—lawless-

ness—freedom—the *natural state* of *nature*—the time before the *world* (state). This time before the world brings with it as it were the scattered features of the *time after the world*—as the state of nature is a *strange picture* of the eternal kingdom. The world of the fairy tale is the *absolutely opposite* world to the world of truth (history)—and just for this reason it is so *absolutely similar* to it—as *chaos* is to *accomplished creation*. (On the *idyll*).

In the *future* world everything is as it is in the *former* world—and *yet everything is quite different*. The *future* world is *reasonable* chaos—chaos which penetrated itself—is inside and outside itself—*chaos* squared or infinity.[8]

The *true fairy tale* must be at once a *prophetic representation*—an ideal representation—an absolutely necessary representation. The maker of true fairy tales is a prophet of the future.

Confessions of a truly synthetic *child*—an ideal child. A child is far cleverer and wiser than an adult—the child must be a thoroughly *ironic* child. The child's games—*imitation* of adults. In time history must become a fairy tale—it will become again what it was in the beginning.

15.   GRAMMAR AND LOGIC. Thinking is speaking. Speaking and doing or acting are one operation that has only been modified.
God said Let there be light and there was light.

16.   THEORY OF THE FUTURE OF HUMANITY. (THEOLOGY) The *theory of the future of humanity* contains all that was foretold by God. Every machine, which now lives by the great *perpetuum mobile* is itself to become the *perpetuum mobile*—every person who lives now by God and through God will himself become God.

17.   METAPHYSICS. If you cannot make your thoughts indirectly (and accidentally) perceptible, then do the reverse—make external things directly (and arbitrarily) perceptible. Which is as much as, if you cannot make your thoughts into external things, then make external things into thoughts. If you could not make a thought into an independent soul which would separate itself from you—and would *now* be *extraneous*—something that is occurring in the outside world, then do the reverse with outside things—and transform them into thoughts.

Both operations are idealistic. Whoever has them both perfectly in his power is the *magical idealist*. Ought not the perfection of each of the two operations be dependent on the other.[9]

The nonself is the original separation—procreation on a grand scale. Medical consequences of this separation. Education of the nonself. One friend educates the other for himself.[10] In an *intelligent* (spiritual) person a *new meaning* is formed with each new appearance—a new tool which can be coaxed in its own way and insulted in its own way (a new kind of pleasing and displeasing).

18.   MUSICAL PHYSICS. The center is a consonant—like the periphery (of the universe).
Contemplation of the world begins in the infinite—absolute descant at the center and moves down the scale. Contemplation of ourselves begins with the infinite, absolute bass at the periphery, and moves up the scale. Absolute uniting of the bass and the descant.[11]
This is the systole and the diastole of divine life.

19.   PHILOSOPHY. To contemplate an object completely means to make it the *center* of my activity. The theory of pure objects is ENCYCLOPEDISTICS like the theory of the heavenly bodies itself—thoroughly mathematical and that is why this spiritual astronomy is so simple. Astronomy is the real algebra of physics—one can even call astronomy the *metaphysics* of nature.[12]
Metaphysics and astronomy are one science. The sun is to astronomy what God is to metaphysics. Freedom and immortality are like light and heat.
God, freedom, and immortality will thus someday become the bases of spiritual physics—just as sun, light, and heat are the bases of earthly physics.

20.   POLITICS. The doctrine of the mediator bears application to politics.[13] Here too the monarch—or government officials—are *representatives of the state—mediators of the state*. What is valid there is valid here. Here the physiological principle is reversed. The more intelligent and lively are the parts—the more lively, the more personal is the state. The *spirit of the state* shines forth from each true citizen of the state—as in a religious community a personal God is revealed as it were in a thousand forms. The state and God, like every spiritual being, do not appear *singly* but in a thousand, manifold forms. Only pantheistically does God appear *wholly*—and only in pantheism is God *wholly* everywhere, in every individual. Thus for the great I, the ordinary I and the ordinary You are only supplements. Every You is a supplement to the great I. We are not I at all—but we can and must become I. We are seeds for becoming I. We

must transform everything into a You—into a second I—only through this do we raise ourselves to the Great I—which is at once *One* and all.[14]

21.   PHILOSOPHICAL TELEOLOGY. Philosophy cannot bake bread—but it can bring us God, freedom, and immortality. Which is more practical then—philosophy or economics?

22.   MISCELLANEOUS. Excitability and sensibility stand in similar relations to each other as soul and body—or spirit and man or world. The world is the *macroanthropos*.[15] It is a world spirit as there is a world soul. The soul is to become spirit—the body to become world. The world is not yet finished—as little as the world spirit is. One God is to become an All-god. From one world—a universe. Higher physics—from common physics. Man is common prose—he is to become higher prose—all-encompassing prose. To cultivate the spirit is to cultivate the world spirit as well—and therefore *religion*. But the spirit is cultivated by the soul— for the soul is nothing but bound, inhibited, consonanted spirit. To cultivate the soul is therefore to cultivate the world spirit as well—and therefore indirectly a religious duty.

23.   PHYSIOLOGY. Imperfect medicine, like imperfect politics, is necessarily bound up with imperfect, *real, present* circumstances (conflict between theory and practice). But it is necessary that scientific ideals are set up—as the necessary bases and beginnings of a future improvement in the subject and the art. Beginning and end are both *ends*.
The senses in the strict sense are much more *animated* than the rest of the organs; the rest of the body must follow them—and they must at the same time become more animated—and so on infinitely. The rest of the body must also become ever more *arbitrary*, as they are. Perhaps now the necessity for *sleep* arises from the disproportion between the senses and the rest of the body. Sleep must compensate the rest of the body for the consequences of excessive stimulation of the senses. Banishment of sleep. (Involuntary—instinctive.) Sleep is peculiar to the dwellers on our planet. Someday the human being will be able constantly to sleep and be awake at the same time. The largest part of our body, our humanity itself, is still sleeping a deep sleep.
Semen is a means of nourishment and stimulation for the woman to replace the menstrua. Thus in the truest sense man lives also for woman.

24.   ENCYCLOPEDISTICS. *Criteria are equal to characteristics.* Hitherto philosophers, like natural scientists, have always begun from single *crite-*

ria. Only *one-sided systematic series* have been constructed—as a single criterion is as it were a logical *unit*—and thus there arose an arithmetical or a gradual (geometrical) systematic series—according as the characteristic was able to be counted or compared (gradual). Many indeed have uncritically chosen several criteria and thence also found themselves with a confused system. A critique of philosophical criteria is therefore of the greatest importance for philosophy—as is a critique of scientific criteria for natural history.

25.   ENCYCLOPEDISTICS. The poet is the inventor of *symptoms* a priori. Since words belong to symptoms, language is a poetic invention—and all revelations and *phenomena,* as symptomatic systems—are poetic in origin—poetics of nature. In the end the philosopher would also be only the inner poet—and so everything real would be thoroughly poetic. Synthetic poetry—*analysis of the external and the internal* at the same time.

26.   PSYCHOLOGY. Faith also has degrees. It orders things. The whole world sprang from the power of faith—it is the *synthetic principle.* Meaning and concept are *one.* A meaning is a *general concept*—that is, an individual concept—not general in the ordinary sense—where it is *polar.* The concept springs from choice—assumption—positing—so too meaning. The foundation of creation lies in the *will.* Faith is the effect of the will on the intelligence—objective and subjective intelligence. The effect of the objective intelligence will be an *object,* a natural being—the effect of the subjective intelligence will be a subject, a concept—a being of the understanding. The power of faith is therefore the will. From the application of this the world gradually arises.

27.   MUSICAL MATHEMATICS. Does not music have something of combinatorial analysis and conversely. Number harmonies—number acoustics—are part of combinatorial analysis.
The numerators are the mathematical vowels—all numbers are *numerators.* Combinatorial analysis leads to improvisation in numbers—and teaches the *numbers the art of composition*—mathematical thorough-bass. Language is a musical instrument of ideas. The poet, rhetorician, and philosopher *play* and compose grammatically. A fugue is thoroughly *logical* or scientific. It can also be treated poetically.
The thorough-bass contains musical algebra and analysis. Combinatorial analysis is critical algebra and analysis—and the theory of musical com-

position stands in the same relation to the *thorough-bass* as combinatorial analysis does to simple analysis.

Many mathematical tasks can be solved not singly but only in combination with others—from a higher point of view—simply through a combinatorial operation.

28.   My book is to become a scientific bible—a real, and ideal, model—and seed of all books.

29.   PHILOSOPHY. It is dogmatic—if I say—there is no God, there is no nonself—there is no thing in itself. Critically I can only say—now there is no such being for me—other than one that is *made up*. All illusion is as essential to the truth as the body is to the soul—error is the necessary instrument of truth. With error I make truth—complete use of error—complete possession of truth.

All synthesis—all progression—or transition begins with *illusion*. I see outside myself what is in me—I believe that what I am doing at the moment has *happened* and so forth. Error of time and space. Faith is the operation of *deception*—the basis of illusion. All knowledge in the distance is faith—the concept outside myself is the thing. All knowledge begins and ends in faith.

30.   COSMOLOGY. The inner world is at it were more mine than the *external*. It is so intimate, so secret. One would like to live wholly in it—it is so like one's homeland. A shame that it is so dreamlike, so uncertain. Must then the best, the truest thing look so feigned—and what is feigned look so true? What is outside me is in me, is mine—and conversely.

31.   COSMOLOGY. Everything is mutually a *symptom*. Sounds and marks, as that *simple*, outward appearance which can be most variously shaped, varied and assembled, can most readily work as the designation of the universe. The universe is the absolute subject or the essence of all predicates. Herein indeed lies its immeasurable and at the same time measurable *structure*, because only through this does the essence of all predicates become possible. One cannot avoid taking fright when one looks into the depths of the spirit. Profundity and the will etc. know no bounds. It is with this as it is with heaven. *Exhausted*, the power of the imagination stands *still*—and only its momentary constitution is thereby indicated. Here we arrive at the possibility of *mental illnesses*—mental weaknesses—in short, at the theory of mental life and constitution—and the moral law appears here as the sole true, great law of the raising of the universe to a higher

degree — as the basic law of harmonious development. Unceasingly man progresses — more easily with each true step — with each new speed that is attained space for movement grows. Only the backwards-directed gaze brings us forwards, since the forwards-directed gaze leads backwards.

PHILOSOPHICAL HISTORIOGRAPHY. Whether the human race is progressing etc. is a strange, *unanswerable*, philosophical question; why not ask also: Does the human race change? This question is higher — a conclusion about improvement or deterioration can only be drawn from change.

COSMOLOGY. It is *all one* whether I posit the universe in myself or myself in the universe. Spinoza posited everything outside — Fichte everything inside. So it is with freedom. If there is freedom in the whole then there is freedom also in me. If I call freedom necessity, and posit necessity in the whole, then necessity is in me and conversely.

32. PHILOSOPHY AND PATHOLOGICAL LOGIC. Note that all treatment of error leads to error. Idealization of realism and realization of idealism leads to truth. One *works* for the *other* — and so indirectly for itself. The idealist, in order to work directly for idealism, must try to prove realism — and conversely. The *proof of realism* is idealism — and conversely. If he wants to prove idealism directly he arrives at zero, that is, he is always turning in a circle — or better, he stays in one place. All proof moves toward the opposite.

Everything is *demonstrable* equals everything is *antinomical*.

There is a sphere where every *proof is a circle* — or an error — where nothing is demonstrable. This sphere is the cultivated golden age. The polar sphere and this one are also in harmony. I realize the golden age — as I develop the polar sphere.[16] I am within it, unconsciously, insofar as I am in the polar sphere unconsciously — and consciously in so far as I am in both consciously.

33. PHILOSOPHICAL PATHOLOGY. An absolute drive toward perfection and completeness is an illness, as soon as it shows itself to be destructive and averse toward the *imperfect*, the incomplete.

If a person wants to do or attain something definite then he must set himself definite limits, even if they are provisional. But whoever does not want to do this is perfect, like someone who does not want to swim until he is able to.

He is a magical idealist, insofar as magical idealists exist. The first person is looking for a wonder movement — a wonder subject — the second a wonder object — a wonder form. Both are *logical illnesses* — kinds of delusion—in which nonetheless the ideal is revealed or reflected in two ways. Holy—isolated beings—who wondrously break up the higher light.[17]

34.   PHILOSOPHY. There is no philosophy *in concreto*. Philosophy is, like the philosopher's stone—squaring the circle etc.—purely a necessary task of the scientist—the *ideal of learning* itself.
That is why Fichte's *Theory of Scientific Knowledge*—is nothing but a *description of this ideal*. As concrete branches of learning there are only *mathematics* and *physics*.
Philosophy is intelligence itself. Perfect philosophy is perfect intelligence.

35.   Every branch of learning becomes poetry—after it has become philosophy.

36.   On dress—as a *symbol*. Clothes in antiquity etc. Clothing is a symbol of the spirit of the times.
Symbolistics forms a part of the study of tropes. Every symbol can be symbolized again by that which it symbolizes—countersymbols. But there are also symbols of symbols—undersymbols.
All the superstition and error of all ages, peoples, and individuals rests on confusion of the *symbol* with what is symbolized—on regarding them as identical—on the belief in genuine, complete representation—and the relation between the image and the original—the appearance and the substance—on inference from external resemblance—on generally acknowledged inner agreement and connection—in short, on repeated confusion of subject and object.

37.   The obsession for originality is scholarly, *coarse* egoism. Anyone who does not treat every extraneous thought like his own, and his own like an extraneous thought—is not a true scholar.
The production of new ideas can become a useless luxury. It is an active collecting—working on what is collected is already a higher degree of activity. For the true scholar there is nothing *of his own* and nothing *extraneous*. To him everything is at once his own and extraneous. To the philosophical body the body itself is extraneous and its own—stimulus and excitability—at the same time.
The scholar knows how to make the extraneous his own and make what is his own extraneous. Learning and teaching—observing and depicting—eating and excreting.

Higher striving after higher originality—even in the world of learning one must *love* and *choose*, in order to be able to exist and enjoy one's being.

38. Everything perfect not only expresses itself—it also expresses a whole related world. That is why the veil of the eternal virgin floats around perfection of every kind—which the lightest touch dissolves in magic fragrance, which becomes the cloud-carriage of the prophet. It is not only antiquity that we see—it is heaven, the telescope—and the fixed star at the same time—and therefore a true revelation of a higher world. One should not believe too rigidly that antiquity and perfection are *made*—made, in the sense that we call made. They are made as the beloved is through the arranged sign of her friend in the night—as the spark is made through the touch of the conductor—or the star through the movement in the eye. In just the same way as the star appears in the *telescope* and penetrates it—so too a *heavenly form* appears in the marble figure.

With every move in perfecting it the work leaps away from the master into more than spatial distances—and thus with the last move the master sees the work that is ostensibly his separated from himself by a gulf of thought—whose breadth he himself can scarcely grasp—and which only the power of the imagination can cross. At the moment when it was to become wholly his it became more than himself, its creator—and he became the unknowing instrument and property of a higher power. The artist belongs to the work and not the work to the artist.

39. Truly abstract or general concepts are differences in the sense of the differential calculus—merely copula.

The *creative power of the imagination* is divided into reason, judgment, and sensory power. Every *conception* (utterance of the productive imagination) is made up of all three—certainly in different relations—types and sizes.

Might certain intellectual limits or imperfections exist because of religion—like helplessness because of love. We have determined to be human beings, in order to be bound in an infinite way even to beings outside our world, and we have *chosen* a god, like a monarch.

Might Fichte in the proposition—the self cannot limit itself—be inconsequential—compliant toward the principle of sufficient cause. The possibility of self-limitation is the possibility of all synthesis—of all miracles and a miracle began the world.

Are synthetic judgments a priori possible is the same as: Is there a magical intelligence, that is, reason.

40.   Strange, contradictory, religious theories of feeling among the *pietists* and *Moravian Brethren*—their relation to mechanics, electricity, and chemistry. (crushing, melting, breaking through)
Kant's lawyer's spirit.[18]
What is *mysticism*—what must be treated *mystically* (mysteriously)?
Religion, love, nature, state.
Everything that is *elect* refers to mysticism. If all human beings were a pair of lovers, the difference between mysticism and nonmysticism would disappear.
Hemsterhuis's theory of a moral sense—his assumptions of perfectibility and the infinitely possible use of this sense. Philosophical ethics—poetic ethics.
Beauty and morality are almost like light and heat in the world of the spirits. Through close knowledge of these—their relationship—their analogy—it will be possible to found and carry out a science of the world of the spirits through beauty and morality as we can a science of the astral world through light and heat.
Does mysticism kill reason? Kant means dogmatism. Dogmatism *cancels out relations* etc. Activity or inactivity.
The theory of religion is learned poetry. Poetry is for the sensations—what philosophy is for the thoughts.
The whole state amounts to representation.
All representation rests on making present that which is not present and so on—marvelous power of *fiction*. My faith and love rests on *representative faith*. Thus the assumption—eternal peace already exists—God is among us—here or nowhere is America—the golden age is here—we are magicians—we are moral and so on.[19]

41.   Time and space come into being together and are therefore probably one, like subject and object. Space is enduring time—time is fluid, variable space. Space—the basis of everything enduring—time—the basis of everything changeable. Space is the schema—time the concept—the action (genesis) of this schema. For every moment my thinking must add a moment before and after.

42.   Actually *criticism*—(or the *exhaustive* method, which comprehends also the antithetical method), that doctrine which in the study of nature directs our attention to ourselves, to inner observation and experiment,

and in the study of ourselves directs it to the outside world, to outer observations and experiments—is philosophically speaking the most fruitful of all *indications.*

It allows us to sense nature, or the *outside world,* as like a human being. It shows that we can and must understand *everything* only as we understand ourselves and our *loved ones,* us and *you.*

Nature is the *ideal.* The true ideal is at once possible, real, and necessary. The principle *self* is *as it were* the true communal and liberal, universal principle—it is a whole, to be without *limit* and regulation. Rather it makes all regulations possible and firm—and gives them absolute continuity and meaning. Selfhood is the foundation of all *knowledge*—as the foundation of the enduring in the changeable—also the principle of the greatest diversity—(you). Instead of nonself—you.

43.   Consideration of the concept of *causality*—the system of transfusion—the system of arousing etc.

A *pure* thought—a *pure* image, a *pure* sensation are thoughts, images, and sensations—which are not aroused etc. through a corresponding object but *have arisen* outside what are called mechanical *laws*—the sphere of mechanism. The imagination is such an extramechanical power. Magical or synthesizing power of the imagination. Philosophy appears here entirely as magical idealism.

44.   Nothing is more Romantic than what we usually call world and destiny. We live in a colossal novel (writ *large* and *small*).

45.   Philosophy is actually homesickness—the *urge to be everywhere at home.*

46.   On our self—as *the flame* of the body in the *soul.* Similarity of the soul to oxygen. Oxygen as a process of irritability. All synthesis is a *flame*—or spark—or analogon of this.

47.   The *proofs* of God perhaps are worth something en masse—as *method.* God here is something like infinity in mathematics—or nought to the power of nought. (*Degrees of zero*) (Philosophy of zero).

(*God* is now one to infinity—now one over infinity—now zero.)

God is a *mixed* concept. It arose from the union of all mental powers etc. by means of a moral revelation, a moral miracle of centering.

God, like philosophy, is each and everything to everyone—*x* personified—Fichte's nonself.

Fichte's nonself is the unity of all stimuli—that which is absolutely stimulating and for just that reason has become like—an eternally unknown. Only *life* stimulates and only life cannot be enjoyed.

48.   A fairy tale is actually like a dream image—without context. An *ensemble* of marvelous things and incidents—for example, a *musical fantasy*—the harmonic products of an Aeolian harp—*nature itself*.
If a *story* is brought into the fairy tale, this is already an alien interference.

49.   Time is *inner space*—space is *outer time*. (Synthesis of these) *Time figures* etc. Space and time originate at the same time.
The energy of temporal individuals is measured *by space*—the energy of spatial individuals by time (*duration*).
Every body has its time—every time has its body. *Time constructions*. (Time triangles—time figuration—time stereometry—time trigonometry.)

50.   All historical scholarship strives to be *mathematical*. Mathematical energy is the *ordering* energy. Every kind of mathematical scholarship strives to become philosophical again—to become *animated* or rationalized—then poetic—finally moral—ultimately *religious*.

51.   On the spirit of *mercantilism*.
The spirit of commerce is the *spirit of the world*. It is the *splendid* spirit itself. It sets everything in motion and combines everything. It wakens countries and cities—nations and works of art. It is the spirit of culture—the perfecting of the human race. The *historical* spirit of commerce—which slavishly follows *given needs*—the circumstances of time and place—is only a bastard of the true, *creative* spirit of commerce.

52.   Philosophy is *antihistorical* from the ground up. It moves from the world of the *future* and the necessary to the real. It is the study of the general sense of *divination*. It explains the past from the future, whereas in history the contrary is the case. *It considers* everything in *isolation*, in the state of nature—unconnected.

53.   The active use of the organs is nothing but *magical, wonder-working* thinking, or *arbitrary* use of the corporeal world—for the will is nothing but the magical, *powerful* capacity for thought.

9 *Christendom or Europe*

There once were beautiful, splendid times when Europe was a Christian land, when *one* Christendom dwelt in this continent, shaped by human hand; *one* great common interest bound together the most distant provinces of this broad religious empire.[1] Although he did not have extensive secular possessions, *one* supreme ruler guided and united the great political powers. A numerous guild which everyone could join ranked immediately below the ruler and carried out his wishes, eagerly striving to secure his beneficent might.[2] Each member of this society was honored on all sides, and whenever the common people sought from him consolation or help, protection or advice, being glad in exchange to provide richly for his diverse needs, each also found protection, esteem, and a hearing from the more mighty ones, while all cared for these chosen men, who were armed with wondrous powers like children of heaven, and whose presence and favor spread many blessings. Childlike trust bound people to their pronouncements. How cheerfully each could accomplish his earthly tasks, since by virtue of these holy people a safe future was prepared for him, and every false step was forgiven by them, and every discolored mark in his life wiped away and made clear. They were the experienced helmsmen on the great unknown sea, under whose protection all storms could be made light of, and one could be confident of a safe arrival and landing on the shore of a world that was truly a fatherland.[3]

The wildest, greediest inclinations had to yield to respect and obedience toward their words. Peace emanated from them. They preached nothing but love for the holy, wonderfully beautiful Lady of Christendom, who, endowed with divine powers, was ready to save every believer from the most terrible dangers.[4] They told of those long dead in heaven, who, through devotion and fidelity to the Blessed Mother and her friendly divine Child, withstood the temptation of the earthly world, achieving honor in the sight of God, and who now have become protective, benevolent forces for their living brethren, willing helpers in need, intercessors on behalf of human failings and efficacious friends of mankind before the heavenly throne. With what serenity one left beautiful gatherings in mysterious churches decorated with inspiring pictures, filled with sweet scents and enlivened by uplifting sacred music. There the sanctified remains of once God-fearing people were gratefully preserved in precious vessels. And there divine goodness and omnipotence and the mighty benevolence of these happy devout ones were revealed in splendid miracles and signs. Thus loving souls preserve locks of hair or the writing of their departed loved ones, and nourish their sweet ardor with these until death reunites them. Objects which had belonged to these beloved souls were collected with devoted care, and those who possessed such a consoling relic or even could only touch it held themselves fortunate. Now and then heavenly grace seemed to have been specially bestowed on a strange picture or a grave-mound. People streamed to that place from all regions with beautiful offerings and brought back heavenly gifts in return: peace of mind and health of body.[5] Tirelessly this mighty peace-making society sought to bring this beautiful faith to all humanity, and sent its fellows to every continent to preach the gospel of life, and to make the kingdom of heaven the only kingdom in this world.[6] With justice, the wise supreme head of the church set himself against the impudent products which arose from human propensities at the expense of the holy message, and against dangerous untimely discoveries in the realm of knowledge. Thus he prevented bold thinkers from publicly asserting that the earth was an insignificant planet, for he well knew that if people lost respect for their own dwelling place and their earthly fatherland, they would also lose respect for their heavenly home and its kind, would give precedence to limited knowledge over eternal faith and become accustomed to scorn everything great and deserving of wonder, regarding it as the lifeless effect of laws.[7] All the clever and venerable men of Europe gathered at his court. All treasures flowed to it, the destruction of Jerusalem had been avenged and Rome itself had become Jerusalem, the holy seat of divine rule on earth. Princes placed their disputes before the father of Christendom, willingly laying their crowns and their glory at his feet, indeed they considered themselves honored to conclude the evening of their lives as members of this high guild, in contemplation of the divine within secluded monastery walls. How beneficial, how suited to the inner nature of man this regime, this arrangement was, was shown by the powerful drive upwards of all other human forces and by the harmonious development of all institutions, the tremendously high attainments reached by individual people in all branches of the study of life and the arts, and the trade in spiritual and earthly goods that flourished everywhere within the bounds of Europe and beyond it to farthest India.[8]

These were the beautiful essential aspects of truly Catholic or truly Christian times. Humanity was not mature enough, not cultivated enough for this splendid kingdom.[9] It was a first love that fell asleep under the pressure of business life, whose memory was supplanted by selfish cares, and whose bond was afterwards berated as deception and delusion and judged according to later experiences, then torn apart forever by a large number of Europeans.[10] This great inner schism, which was accompanied by destructive wars, was a remarkable sign of the harmfulness of civilization to the meaning of the invisible, at least of a temporary harmfulness of civilization at a certain stage. That immortal meaning cannot be destroyed, but it can be confused, paralyzed, supplanted by other meanings. A more enduring community of people confines its inclinations and the belief in its own kind, and accustoms itself to apply all its endeavors only to the means of attaining its well-being; their requirements and the art of satisfying them become more complicated, the acquisitive person needs so much time to become acquainted with these and to acquire skills in them that there is no time left for quietly gathering his thoughts or for the attentive contemplation of the inner world. When clashes occur, the present interest seems to him to be more pressing, and thus the lovely blossom of his youth, faith and love, falls and gives way to the more bitter fruits of knowing and possessing.[11] In late autumn we think of spring as if it were a childish dream, and hope with childish simplicity that the full storerooms will last forever. A certain solitariness seems to be necessary if the higher senses are to flourish, hence too extensive social intercourse of people with each other must choke many a holy seed and frighten away the gods, who flee from the restless tumult of distracting social occasions and negotiations of petty matters.[12] Moreover, we are concerned with ages and periods, and is not an oscillation, an alternation of opposite movements essential to these? is not limited existence proper to them, is not their nature growth and decline? But can we not also expect with certainty that they will be resurrected and rejuvenated in a new, vigorous form? Progressive, ever-expanding evolutions are the stuff of history.[13] That which does not achieve perfection now will achieve it at some future attempt or the next; nothing captured by history is ephemeral, from countless transformations it comes forth renewed in ever richer forms. But once Christianity had appeared in its full might and splendor, its ruin, the letter of it, reigned with ever-increasing impotence and mockery until the appearance of a new world inspiration. Infinite lethargy lay heavily on the members of the clerical guild, who had become complacent. They had stuck fast in the sense of their own importance and comfort, while the laymen had stolen their experience and learning from under their very eyes and taken mighty steps forward on the way to education. Forgetting their proper office of being the first among men in spirit, insight, and education, they had allowed base desires to overcome them, and the vulgarity and baseness of their thinking became even more repulsive because of their dress and their profession. Thus respect and confidence, the pillars of this and of every kingdom, gradually fell away, and as a result that guild was destroyed, and the proper rule of Rome had silently ceased to exist long before the violent insurrection. Only clever and thus also only earthly measures still held the corpse of the order together and protected it against too swift a dissolution, which was deserved above all, for example, by the abolition of marriage for priests. This is a measure which, analogously applied, could also lend fearful consistency to the similar class of soldiers and blight its existence for yet many a day. What was more natural than that finally a fiery hothead should preach public rebellion against the despotic letter of the former order, and that with the greater success since he was himself a member of the guild.[14]

The insurgents rightly called themselves Protestants, for they were protesting solemnly against every unjust presumption about conscience made by a troublesome and seemingly unjust power. They provisionally reclaimed for themselves as vacant the right to religious inquiry, determination, and choice, which they had earlier silently surrendered. They also set up many just principles, introduced many praiseworthy things and abolished many pernicious precepts; but they forgot the necessary result of their process; they separated what cannot be separated, divided the indivisible Church and tore themselves unlawfully out of the general Christian communion, through which and in which alone a true, enduring rebirth was possible. The state of religious anarchy must be only temporary, for the essential reason for dedicating a number of people purely to this high calling, and making these people independent of earthly power in respect of these matters, remains enduringly effective and valid. The establishment of the consistories and the retention of a kind of clergy did not obviate this need, and was not an adequate substitute. Unhappily the princes had intervened in this schism, and many of them used these disputes to strengthen and extend their power and income as provincial rulers. They were glad to be relieved of that high influence and now took the new consistories under their own patronage and direction. They were most zealously concerned to prevent the complete unification of the Protestant churches, and thus in a most irreligious manner religion was confined within national borders, thereby laying the foundation for the gradual undermining of cosmopolitan religious interest. In this way religion lost its great political influence as a peacemaker, its particular role as a unifying, individualizing principle, as Christendom itself. Religious peace was concluded on quite faulty and counterreligious foundations, and something thoroughly contradictory—a revolutionary government— was declared permanent as a result of the continuation of what is called Protestantism.

Meanwhile, Protestantism is far from being based only on that pure concept, but rather Luther treated Christianity altogether as he pleased, mistook its spirit and introduced another letter and another religion, namely the holy universal validity of the Bible, whereby unfortunately another extremely alien aspect of secular learning was introduced into the matter of religion—philology—whose all-consuming influence becomes unmistakable from that moment onward. He himself, given only a dim sense of this error on the part of a large number of Protestants, was raised to the level of an evangelist and his translation canonized.[15]

This choice was highly damaging to the religious sense, since nothing destroys its responsiveness so much as the letter itself. In the circumstances that had obtained formerly, given the comprehensive suppleness and rich substance of the Catholic faith, together with the fact that the Bible as well as the holy power of the Councils and the supreme spiritual ruler were held to be esoteric, the letter itself could never become so harmful; but now these countermeasures were destroyed, the absolute popularity of the Bible was asserted, and now the inadequate content, the rough, abstract sketch of religion in these books was all the more noticeably oppressive, and made it infinitely difficult for the Holy Spirit to bring about free vivification, penetration, and revelation.

That is also why the history of Protestantism shows us no more splendid great visions of the supernatural, only its beginning shines through a transient heavenly fire, soon afterwards it is already noticeable that the holy message is drying up; the secular has gained the upper hand, the understanding of art suffers in sympathy, only rarely does a sturdy, eternal spark of life leap forth and a small community comes together. When the spark is extinguished the community dissipates and is washed away with the tide. So it was with Zinzendorf, Jacob Böhme, and several others.[16] The moderatists retain the upper hand, and the time of a total loss of muscle tone in the higher organs is approaching, the period of practical unbelief. With the Reformation it was all up with Christendom. From then on it did not exist anymore. Catholics and Protestants or members of the Reformed Church were more radically cut off from each other by sectarian differences than Mohammedans and heathens. The remaining Catholic states continued to vegetate, not without imperceptibly feeling the harmful influence of the neighboring Protestant states. Recent politics stem only from this moment, when single powerful states sought to take possession of the vacant universal seat, now transformed into a throne.

Most princes felt it a humiliation to be constrained by a powerless cleric. For the first time they felt the weight of their physical power on earth, saw the heavenly powers idle as their representatives were insulted, and now sought little by little and without attracting the attention of their subjects, who were still eager adherents of the papacy, to throw off the burdensome Roman yoke and make themselves independent on earth. Their uneasy consciences were laid to rest by clever spiritual advisers, who lost nothing by the fact that their spiritual children dared to assume the disposition of Church wealth.

Fortunately for the old confession a newly founded order now came forward, on which the dying spirit of the hierarchy seemed to have showered its last gifts, an order which girded the old with new strength, and with marvelous insight and perseverance, more cleverly than any before it, took up the cause of the papal empire and its regeneration in a more powerful form.[17] Never before in the history of the world had such a society been encountered. Even the ancient Roman senate had not drawn up plans to conquer the world with greater assurance of success. Never had the implementation of a greater idea been conceived with greater understanding. This society will remain forever a model for all societies which feel an organic yearning to expand infinitely and to endure forever, but also it will remain forever as proof that unguarded time alone makes the cleverest undertakings vain, and the natural growth of the whole race inevitably suppresses the artificial growth of a part of it. Everything that exists singly has its own measure of ability, only the capacity of the race is immeasurable. All plans are doomed to fail that do not fully rest on all the propensities of the race. This society becomes even more remarkable as the mother of what are called secret societies, of an as yet still immature but assuredly important historical seed.[18] The new Lutheranism, not Protestantism, certainly could not have acquired a more dangerous rival. All the magic of the Catholic faith became even more vigorous in their hands, the treasures of learning flowed back into their cells. What was lost in Europe they sought to regain in many other parts of the world, in the farthest Occident and Orient, striving to make the apostolic dignity and profession their own and lend it validity. They too were not tardy in striving for popularity, and knew well how much Luther had owed to his demagogic skills and his study of the common people. Everywhere they established schools, pushed into the confessionals, climbed into the pulpits and employed the printing presses, became poets and men of the world, ministers and martyrs, and even in their massive expansion from America through Europe to China they remained in the most marvelous concord in deed and doctrine. Wisely they chose recruits for their order from their own schools. They preached against the Lutherans with destructive zeal and sought to make it the most pressing duty of Catholic Christendom to stamp out these heretics most cruelly as authentic comrades-in-arms of the devil. The Catholic states and in particular the papal throne had only them to thank for their long survival of the Reformation, and who knows how old the world would still be looking had not weak generals, the jealousy of the princes and of other holy orders, court intrigues and other special circumstances interrupted their bold progress and almost destroyed with them this last bastion of Catholic teaching. Now it is asleep, this terrible order, in pitiful shape on the borders of Europe, perhaps one day, like the common people who protect it, it will spread out thence with new force across its old homeland, perhaps under another name.[19]

The Reformation had been a sign of the times. It was significant for the whole of Europe even though it had broken out publicly only in Germany, since this was truly free. Sensible people of all nations had secretly attained their majority, and deceived by a sense of their calling they rose up the more vigorously against a compulsion which had become obsolete. The scholar is by instinct the enemy of the clergy of the old kind; the scholarly and clerical classes must needs wage wars of extermination if they are separate; for they are fighting for one place. This separation became ever more marked, and the more the clerical element of European humanity approached the period of triumphant scholarship, the more the scholars gained ground, and knowledge and faith moved into more decisive opposition. The reason for the general stagnation was sought in the faith, and it was hoped to alleviate this through the pervasive effect of knowledge.[20] Everywhere the holy message suffered under manifold persecutions of the style it had hitherto displayed, its mature personality. The product of the modern way of thinking was called philosophy, and it was held to embrace everything that was opposed to the old way, principally therefore every objection to religion. What was at first personal hatred of the Catholic faith gradually turned into hatred of the Bible, of the Christian faith and finally even of religion. Still more — hatred of religion extended itself very naturally and consequentially to all the objects of enthusiasm, made heretics of imagination and feeling, rectitude and love of art, the past and the future, it just managed to place mankind at the head of the series of natural beings, and turned the infinite, creative music of the universe into the uniform clattering of a monstrous mill, driven by the stream of chance and floating on it, a mill of itself without builder or miller and really a true *perpetuum mobile*, a mill grinding itself.[21]

One enthusiasm was generously left for the poor human race and made indispensable as a touchstone of the highest education for every practitioner of it. It was enthusiasm for this splendid, magnificent philosophy and in particular for its priests and mystagogues. France was fortunate enough to become the birthplace and the seat of this new faith, that was stuck together out of nothing but knowledge. However much poetry was decried in this new church, there were still some poets in it who continued to make use of the old ornaments and the old candles for effect, but in doing so risked setting the new world system alight with old fire. Cleverer church members, however, knew at once that the listeners, who had already warmed to what they were hearing, must be doused with cold water again. These members were tirelessly engaged in cleansing nature, the earth, human souls, and learning of poetry, rooting out every trace of the sacred, spoiling the memory of all uplifting incidents and people by sarcastic remarks, and stripping the world of all bright ornament. Because of its mathematical obedience and its boldness, light had become their darling. They were pleased that it would rather allow itself to be shattered than play with colors, and thus they named their great task after it, Enlightenment.[22] In Germany this task was pursued more thoroughly, the system of education was reformed, an attempt was made to give the old religion a newer, rational, more common meaning, by carefully washing away from it all the wonder and mystery; all available learning was summoned to cut off the flight to history, while it was attempted to refine history so that it might become a portrait of domestic and bourgeois moral and family life.[23] God was turned into an idle spectator of the great, moving spectacle performed by the scholars, a spectator who in the end was supposed to receive the poets and players ceremonially with hospitality and admiration. The common people enjoyed some preference in being enlightened, and were trained to adopt that cultivated enthusiasm, and thus there arose a new guild of Europeans: the philanthropists and Enlighteners. What a shame that nature remained so marvelous and incomprehensible, so poetic and infinite, in spite of all efforts to modernize it. If somewhere an old superstitious belief in a higher world and suchlike reared its head, the alarm was sounded at once on all sides, and whenever possible the dangerous spark was suffocated in the ashes by philosophy and wit;[24] nonetheless tolerance was the slogan of the educated, and particularly in France was equated with philosophy. This history of modern unbelief is extremely strange, and is the key to all the monstrous phenomena of recent times. It does not begin until this century and especially during its second half, then it grows in a short time to immeasurable size and diversity; a second Reformation, a more comprehensive and particular one was unavoidable, and had to strike first that country which was most modernized, and which had lain the longest in a condition of asthenia as a result of lack of freedom.[25] The supernatural fire would long since have flared up and thwarted the clever Enlightenment plans, had not secular pressure and influence stood the latter in good stead. But at the very moment when a dispute arose among the scholars and governments, among the enemies of religion and all their associates, it was obliged to step forward again as a third influential, mediating element, and each of its friends had to acknowledge and proclaim this appearance should it not be sufficiently noticeable. That the time of its resurrection has come, and that just those incidents that seemed to be directed against its enlivening and threatened to complete its demise have now become the most favorable signs of its regeneration, can no longer remain a matter of doubt for any historical mind. True anarchy is the element within which religion is born. From the destruction of everything positive it lifts its glorious head as the founder of a new world. Man rises up toward heaven as if of himself when nothing more binds him, the higher organs step forth of themselves from the general uniform mixture and from the complete dissolution of all human propensities and powers, to appear for the first time as the orig- inal seed of mortal shape. The spirit of God moves across the waters and across the ebbing waves a heavenly island can be seen for the first time as the dwelling place of the new man, as the river zone of eternal life.

Let the genuine observer contemplate the new revolutionary times calmly and without prejudice. Does not the revolutionary seem to him like Sisyphus? Now he has reached the zenith of his equilibrium and already the mighty burden is rolling down again on the other side. It will never stay up unless a force attracting it toward heaven keeps it balanced at the highest point.[26] All your props are too weak if your state still tends toward the earth, but bind it by a higher longing to the heavenly heights and give it a connection to the universe, then you will never have a slack- ening spring within it and you will see your efforts richly rewarded. I direct your attention to history, search in its instructive context for similar moments, and learn to use the magic wand of analogy.

France champions secular Protestantism. Might not secular Jesuits now arise, and the history of the past centuries be renewed? Is the Revolution to remain French as the Reformation was Lutheran? Is Protestantism once more to be established contrary to nature as a revolu- tionary government? Is the letter of the old to give way to the letter of the new? Are you seeking the germ of corruption even in the old institution, the old spirit? and do you believe yourself possessed of a better institution, a better spirit? O! that you were filled with the spirit of spirits and might desist from this foolish striving to mold history and humanity and give them your own direction. Is not history independent, self-reliant, as good as infinitely lovable and prophetic? To study it, follow it, learn from it, keep in step with it, faithfully obeying its promises and its guidance—no one thinks of that.

Much has been done for religion in France by depriving it of the right of citizenship, and leaving it with only the right of abode, and that not as one person but in all its countless individual forms. As a strange unprepossessing orphan, it first had to win back people's hearts and be everywhere loved, before it could again be publicly worshiped and intro- duced into secular matters for friendly counsel and encouragement of minds. The attempt of that great iron mask, which under the name of

Robespierre sought in religion the center and the strength of the republic, remains historically remarkable;[27] so also the coldness with which theophilanthropy, this mysticism of the later Enlightenment, was taken up;[28] also the new conquests of the Jesuits; also the approach to the Orient through recent political relations.[29]

With regard to the European countries other than Germany, one can only prophesy that with *peace* a new, higher, religious life will begin to pulsate in them and will soon swallow up all other secular interest. In Germany, on the other hand, one can already point with complete certainty to traces of a new world. Germany is treading a slow but sure path ahead of the other European countries. While the latter are busy with war, speculation, and partisan spirit, the German is educating himself with all diligence to participate in a higher cultural epoch, and in the course of time this advance must give him much superiority over the others.[30] A tremendous ferment in the arts and sciences is becoming apparent. An infinite amount of intellectual spirit is being developed. New, fresh seams are being mined. The different branches of learning were never in better hands, or at least they never aroused higher expectations; the most diverse properties of objects are being tracked down, there is nothing that is not shaken, assessed, investigated. Everything is worked over; writers are becoming more particular and more powerful, every old monument of history, every art, every science finds friends and is embraced with new love and made fruitful. Incomparable versatility, marvelous depth, lustrous polish, comprehensive knowledge, and a rich, vigorous imagination can be found here and there, often boldly linked together. Everywhere there seems to be stirring a mighty sense of creative will, of limitlessness, of infinite diversity, of holy particularity, and the infinite capacity of the human spirit. Having awoken from the morning dream of helpless childhood, a part of the race is exercizing its first powers on the snakes that entwine its cradle and want to rob it of the use of its limbs.[31] All these things are still only hints, disjointed and rough, but to the historical eye they betray a universal individuality, a new history, a new humanity, the sweetest embrace of a surprised, young church and a loving God, and the ardent conception of a new messiah in all its thousand members at once. Who does not feel the sweet shame of being with child? The newborn will be the image of his father, a new golden age with dark infinite eyes, a prophetic, consoling time, working miracles and healing wounds, and sparking the flame of eternal life—a great time of reconciliation, a savior who like a true genius will be at home among men, who can only be believed in and not seen, and who is visible to the faithful in countless forms, consumed as bread and wine, embraced like a beloved woman, breathed as air, heard as word and song, and with heavenly delight, amid the sharpest pangs of love, taken up in the form of death into the innermost part of the body whose turbulence ceases at last.[32]

Now we are standing high enough to smile kindly even on those times past that were mentioned before, and even to recognize in those strange follies remarkable crystallizations of the historical substance. Gratefully we wish to shake the hands of those scholars and philosophers; for this delusion had to be exhausted for the benefit of posterity, and the scientific aspect of things made valid. Then poetry, like a bejeweled India, will stand more captivatingly and more colorfully over against the cold, dead Spitzbergen of that stuffy understanding. For India to be so warm and splendid in the middle of the globe, both ends of it must be made inhospitable by a cold, rigid sea, dead cliffs, fog instead of the starry heavens, and a long night. The profound meaning of mechanics lay heavily on these anchorites in the deserts of the understanding;[33] the captivating aspect of their first insight overwhelmed them, the old order avenged itself on them, with marvelous self-denial they sacrificed the most sacred and beautiful aspect of the world to their first self-consciousness, and they were the first who once more recognized and heralded the sacredness of nature, the infinity of art, the necessity of knowledge, respect for the secular, and the omnipresence of the truly historical through the deed, and put an end to a higher, more general and more terrible reign of ghosts than they believed themselves.

Only through closer familiarity with religion will one be better able to judge those fearful products of the sleep of religion, those dreams and deliriums of the holy instrument, and then for the first time to learn true insight into the importance of that gift. Where there are no gods, ghosts reign, and the actual period of origin of ghosts in Europe, which also explains their shape almost completely, is the period of transition from the doctrine of the Greek gods to Christianity.[34] So come then you too, all you philanthropists and encyclopedists, into the peace-bringing lodge and receive the fraternal kiss, brush the gray net aside and gaze with young love at the wondrous splendor of nature, history, and humanity.[35] I want to conduct you to a brother who will talk with you so that your hearts rejoice and you gird your beloved, expired sensation with a new body, you once again embrace and recognize what you envisioned, and what ponderous, mortal understanding was indeed not able to seize from you.

This brother is the heartbeat of the new age, whoever has felt his presence does not doubt any more that it will come, and he too steps out from the crowd with sweet pride in being a contemporary to join the new band of disciples. He has made a new veil for the Holy Virgin which caresses her body, betraying the heavenly shape of her limbs, and yet covers her more chastely than any other.[36] The veil is for the Virgin what the spirit is for the body, her indispensable instrument whose folds are the letters of her sweet Annunciation; the infinite play of the folds is a music of numbers, for language is too wooden and too impudent for the Virgin, her lips open only to sing. For me her singing is nothing but the ceremonial call to a new foundation gathering, the mighty beating of the wings of an angelic herald who is passing. They are the first birth-pangs, let everyone prepare for the birth!

The highest achievement in physics is now to hand and so it is easier for us to oversee the scientific guild.[37] In recent times the poverty of the physical sciences has become ever more apparent, the more familiar we have become with them. Nature began to look ever more impoverished until, accustomed to the brilliance of our discoveries, we saw the more clearly that it was only a borrowed light, and that with the familiar tools and the familiar methods we would not find and construct the essential thing we sought. Every researcher had to confess to himself that one science is nothing without the other, and thus there arose attempts at mystification of the sciences, and the strange being of philosophy, a scientific element that had existed purely as representation, now turned out to be a symmetrical basic figure of the sciences. Others brought the concrete sciences into new relations, promoted lively exchanges between them, and sought to clarify their scientific classification. Thus it continues, and it is easy to estimate how advantageous this association with the external and internal world, with the higher cultivation of the understanding, with knowledge of the external world and with stimulus and cultivation of the internal world must be, and how in these circumstances the storm clouds are clearing and the old heavens and with them the longing for them, living astronomy, must once more come forth.

Now we want to turn to the political spectacle of our time. The old and new worlds are locked in conflict, the failings and deficiencies of public institutions that have existed hitherto have become manifest in terrible phenomena. What if it should be the case that here too, as in the sciences, closer and more diverse connection and contact between the states of Europe were in the first instance to be the historical purpose of war, if a new stirring of Europe that had hitherto been asleep were to come into play, if Europe were to awaken again, if a state of states, a political theory of scientific knowledge, were to stand before us![38] Might the hierarchy perhaps be this symmetrical basic figure of the states, the principle of the union of states as the intellectual perception of the political self? It is impossible that secular powers can achieve equilibrium by themselves, only a third element which is at once secular and supernatural can accomplish this task. No peace can be concluded among the warring powers, all peace is only an illusion, only a truce; from the standpoint of the cabinets or of common consciousness unification is unthinkable. Both parties have great, essential claims and must press them, driven by the spirit of the world and of humanity. Both are ineradicable powers of the human heart: on the one hand reverence for antiquity, devotion to historical custom, love of the monuments of our forefathers and the glorious old state family, and joy in obedience; on the other hand the delightful feeling of freedom, the unconditional expectation of mighty spheres of influence, pleasure in the new and young, untrammeled contact with all fellow members of the state, pride in the universal validity of the human, joy in personal rights and in the property of the whole, and a vigorous sense of citizenship. Let no power hope to destroy the other, all conquests mean nothing here, for the innermost capital of each empire does not lie behind fortified walls and cannot be stormed.

Who knows if there has been enough of war, but it will never cease if we do not seize the palm which only a spiritual power can confer. Blood will flow across Europe until the nations become aware of the terrible madness which drives them around in circles and until, affected and soothed by holy music, all in a varied group they approach their former altars to undertake the work of peace, and as a festival of peace a great love feast will be celebrated with warm tears as smoke rises from the sacred places. Only religion can awaken Europe again and make the peoples secure, and with new splendor install Christendom visibly on earth once more in its old peace-bringing office.

Do the nations have everything of man—except his heart? his holy organ? Do they not become friends, as these do, on the coffins of their loved ones, do they not forget all hostility when divine compassion speaks to them—even if one misfortune, one sorrow, one feeling should fill their eyes with tears? Are they not powerfully seized with the spirit of sacrifice and surrender, and do they not yearn to be friends and allies?

Where is that old, dear faith in the kingdom of God on earth which alone can bring salvation, where is that heavenly trust of people in each other, that sweet devotion at the outpourings of a heart inspired by God, that all-embracing spirit of Christendom?

Christianity has three forms. One is the generative element of religion, namely joy in all religion. One is the notion of mediation itself, namely faith in the omnipotence of all earthly things to be the bread and wine of eternal life. One is the faith in Christ, his mother and the saints. Choose whichever you will, choose all three, it is all the same, you will become Christians thereby and members of one single, eternal, inexpressibly happy community.

The old Catholic faith was the last of these forms, it was applied Christianity, a faith that had come alive. Its presence in all aspects of life, its love of art, its deep humanity, the indissolubility of its marriages, its generous openness, its joy in poverty, obedience, and fidelity make it unmistakable as the true religion and embody the basic characteristics of its doctrine.

It is made clean by the river of time; in close, inseparable union with the two other forms of Christianity it will forever bless this earth.

Its incidental form is as good as destroyed, the old papacy lies in its grave and Rome has become a ruin for the second time.[39] Will not Protestantism come to an end at last and make way for a new, more enduring Church? The other continents are awaiting Europe's reconciliation and resurrection so that they might follow and also become citizens of the kingdom of heaven. Might there not soon be many truly holy hearts in Europe again, might not all who are truly close to religion become full of longing to behold heaven on earth? and come gladly together and lift their voice in holy choirs?

Christendom must again become lively and effective, and again form a visible Church without regard to national borders, one which will take up into its bosom all those souls who thirst for the supernatural, and gladly become the mediator between the old world and the new.

It must once again pour out the old cornucopia of blessing on the peoples. Christianity will rise again from the sacred bosom of a venerable European council, and the business of reawakening religion according to an all-embracing divine plan will be undertaken. Then no one will protest any more against Christian and secular constraint, for the essence of the Church will be true freedom, and all necessary reforms will be carried out under its direction, as peaceful and formal processes of state.

When and when sooner? that cannot be asked. Just be patient, it will, it must come, the holy time of eternal peace, when the new Jerusalem will be the capital of the world; and until then, fellow believers, be cheerful and courageous amid the dangers of the time, preach the divine Gospel in word and deed, and cleave to the true, eternal faith until death.

10 *Last Fragments*

1. Elements of the Romantic.[1] Objects must exist at once, like the sounds of the Aeolian harp, without cause—without betraying their instrument.

2. Physics is nothing but the theory of the *imagination.* SEE PATAPHYSICS
   as SOLUTION

3. A novel must be poetry through and through. For poetry, like philosophy, must be a harmonious mood of our mind, where everything is made beautiful, where everything finds its proper aspect—everything finds an *accompaniment* and *surroundings* that suit it. Everything in a truly poetic book seems so *natural*—and yet so marvelous. We think it could not be otherwise, and as if we had only been asleep in the world before now— and now for the first time the right meaning for the world dawns on us. All memory and intimation seems to come from just this source—so too that present where we are caught up in illusion. Single hours where we find ourselves as it were in all the objects that we are contemplating, and we feel the infinite, incomprehensible simultaneous sensations of a plurality in agreement.

4. Fichte's whole philosophy follows necessarily from his presupposition of logic—and his assumption of one generally valid thought. The theory of scientific knowledge is applied logic—nothing more. Philosophy begins with such pusillanimity, a trivial thought—that belongs to its being. It begins with a breath.
The theory of scientific knowledge is nothing but a proof of the *reality of logic*—its agreement with the rest of nature and quite analogously with

153

mathematics in respect of its discoveries and justifications—and of that which it can achieve.

5.   Death is the Romanticizing principle of our life. Death is minus, life is plus.[2] Life is strengthened through death.

6.   One urge seems to me to be generally widespread in our time—to hide the external world under artificial covers—to be ashamed of open nature and to endow it with a dark, ghostly force through making sensuous beings secret and hidden. This urge is assuredly Romantic—but not favorable to childlike innocence and transparency. This is particularly noticeable in sexual relations.

7.   Sound seems to be nothing but a broken movement, in the sense that color is broken light.
Dance is most closely connected with music and like its other half.
Sound is connected with movement as if of itself.
Color is like a neutral condition of matter and light—a striving of matter to become light—and a contrary striving of light.
Might all quality be a *broken* condition—in the above meaning?
Pleasure in diversity of movements.
Might the forms of crystallization—be a *broken* type of gravity?
Influence of mixture on shaping of figures.
Could not crystalline forms be of electrical *origin*?

8.   *Successive* construction through *speech,* and *resonance.* The effect of speech rests on the memory—oratory teaches the rules of the *sequence* of thoughts to achieve a certain intention.[3] Every speech first sets the thoughts in motion and is organized in such a way that one can place the fingers of thought in the easiest order on certain spots.

9.   The art of creative writing is probably only—the arbitrary, active, productive use of our organs—and perhaps thinking itself might be not much else—and thinking and writing are therefore the same thing. For in thinking the senses apply the richness of their impressions to a new kind of impression—and what arises from that we call thoughts.

10.   *Musical relations* seem to me to be actually the basic relations of nature.
Crystallizations: acoustic figures of *chemical oscillations.* (chemical sense)

Brilliant, noble, divinatory, miracle-working, clever, stupid etc. plants, animals, stones, elements etc. *Infinite individuality* of these beings—their musical sense, and sense of individuality—their character—their inclinations etc.

They are *past, historical* beings. Nature is a magic city turned to stone.

11.   Sermons ought actually to be called *legends*, for the actual material of sermons is *legendary material*.[4]

One must seek *God* among men. In human incidents, human thoughts and sensations, the spirit of heaven reveals itself most brightly.

Religious doctrine is quite cut off from this. It can only be understandable and religiously useful to religious people.

One cannot proclaim religion any more than one does *love* and *patriotism*. If one wanted to make someone fall in love, how would one begin to do that?

12.   Doing philosophy is only a threefold or double kind of *waking—being awake—consciousness*.

13.   Strange that up to now the inner world of a person has been observed so inadequately and treated so unimaginatively. What is called psychology is one of those masks which have taken over the places in the sanctuary where real images of the gods ought to be. How little has physics yet been used for the mind—and the mind for the outer world. Understanding, imagination—reason—those are the inadequate products of the universe within us. No word about their marvelous combinations, shapes, transitions. It did not occur to anyone—to seek out new, as yet unknown forces—to track down their sociable relations. Who knows what marvelous unions, what marvelous generations still lie before us in our inner world.

14.   A genuine *love* for a lifeless thing is certainly conceivable—also for plants, animals, for nature—indeed for oneself. As soon as a person has a genuine inner You—then a highly spiritual and sensuous intercourse and the most violent passion is possible—perhaps genius is nothing but the result of such an inner plurality. The secrets of this intercourse are still very much without illumination.

15.   What is it that shapes a person if it is not his *life history*? And in the same way a splendid person is shaped by nothing other than *world history*. Many people live better in the past and the future than in the *present*.

Even the present cannot at all be understood without the *past* and without a high degree of education—saturation with the highest products, the purest spirit of the age and of the past, and a digestion of this, from what source the human prophetic view arises, which the historian, the active, idealistic person who works with the data of history can as little do without as the grammatical and rhetorical storyteller.

In his discourse the historian must often become an orator. Indeed he speaks *gospels*, for the whole of history is gospel.

16.   The preacher must first try to arouse enthusiasm—for this is the *element of religion*. Every word must be clear, warm, and heartfelt. He must seek to *isolate* his congregation in the world—to give them *esprit de corps*—to enlighten them about the world and the higher classes and to *elevate* them—to make their occupation dear to them and their life pleasant and to fill them *with a noble sense of self*.

17.   General statements are not valid in the study of nature. Its discourse must be *practical, technical, real*—developing step-by-step—constructively, like the description of a technical task.

Present-day physics is very inadequate—our physics only speaks about the general elements of nature—of the general *effective concepts*—or the forces of nature. It is a metaphysics or logic of the real world. Plants, animals, stars, human beings are already assembled products of nature—higher natures. Nature is a church of infinite natures. Everything is limited, even human learning must be determined according to time and place etc. Man cannot achieve anything higher than realizing which knowledge is just right for his stage—for the persistence and constitution of his life—if he does not obsessively indulge the thirst for knowledge—but allows it to be in harmony with the rest of his powers and dispositions.

Man is not called to learning only—man must be *man*—he is called to humanity—the tendency to the universal is indispensable for the true scholar. But man must never seek something indeterminate—an ideal, like a fantast—a child of fantasy. He must proceed only from one determinate task to another. An unknown beloved certainly has a magical attraction. Striving for the unknown—the indeterminate—is extremely dangerous and disadvantageous. Revelations cannot be compelled by force.

The truly idealistic path of the physicist is not to explain what is assembled, combined from what is simple, fragmented, but the contrary. A political state will never arise from a state of nature — but a state of nature can well arise from a political state. Nature arose through degeneration. Gravity is explained by the power of sensation — not electricity etc., sensation — by gravity. The origin of gravity is explained by thoughts. The first chapter in physics belongs to the spirit world. Nature cannot be explained as static — it can only be explained as *progressing* — toward morality.

One day there will be no nature anymore — it will gradually turn into a spirit world. Might not the immutable laws of nature be deception — might they not be highly unnatural.

Everything follows laws and nothing follows laws.

A law is a simple, easily overlooked relation.

We seek laws for the sake of convenience. Has not nature a particular will — or none at all? I believe it has both. It is everything to all men.

18. One phenomenon must necessarily lead to other phenomena, as one experiment does to several experiments. Nature is a *whole* — in which each part in itself can never be wholly understood. The true student of nature begins from any point and pursues his path step-by-step into the immeasurable distance with a careful connection and alignment of the individual facts.

Thus, for example, pursuit of the process of combustion.

19. One can produce stimulus or activity merely through altering the links in the chain. Everything is a link in a chain. Each new link causes *representations* in the other links — thereby activity. Each one, it is true, does not invariably cause the required degree of stimulus or activity.

Galvanism explains an enormous amount in animal economy, for example, the system of congestions, evacuations — of double excitability.[5]

One observation has been important for me here — the behavior of the soul in order to express feelings. It seems to do this merely through associations. If the usual associations are no use, then unusual associations help — for example, in arousal of the sexual organs.

20. In the formation of thoughts all parts of the body seem to me to be working together. They seem equally to be results of action and reaction — and from these come the necessary effect of *changed trains of thought*, the *friendly response of others* — apt, pithy remarks — sudden ideas, on the condition of the body. Even in a condition of anxiety and perturbation the soul strives for what is new — often for what is old — in short, for something *different*.

Thus even a fright can have an advantageous effect.

21. Does not language also have its descant and bass and tenor sounds? Its rhythm—a ground tone—diverse voices and tempi? Are not the different kinds of style different instruments?

22. On the *poetry* of nature—the blossom is quite *poetic*.

23. *Wilhelm Meister's Apprenticeship* is to a certain extent thoroughly *prosaic*—and modern.[6] The Romantic quality is destroyed in it—also the nature poetry, the marvelous. He deals with merely ordinary, *human* things—nature and mysticism are quite forgotten. It is a poeticized bourgeois and domestic story. The marvelous element in it is expressly treated as poetic and eccentric. Artistic atheism is the spirit of the book.
Very much economy—a poetic effect achieved with prosaic, cheap material.

24. The similarity of our sacred history with *fairy tale* is extremely strange—at the beginning an enchantment—then the marvelous reconciliation etc. The fulfilment of the magical condition—madness and enchantment are very similar. A magician is an artist of madness.

25. Poetry must never be the main material, always only what is marvelous.
One ought to *represent* nothing which one would not be able to see in its entirety, perceive clearly and be fully master of—for example, in *representations of the supernatural.*

26. Poetry is true idealism—contemplation of the world as one would contemplate a *great mind*—self-consciousness of the universe.

27. A writer needs a calm, alert temperament—ideas or inclinations which keep him from mundane business and petty matters, a situation without care—journeys—acquaintance with many kinds of people—diverse opinions—*freedom from care*—memory—a gift for speaking—no attachment to one object, no passion strictly speaking—all-round receptiveness.

28. *Against Wilhelm Meister's Apprenticeship.* It is at bottom a fatal and foolish book—so pretentious and precious—unpoetic to the highest degree, as far as the spirit is concerned—however poetic the description. It is a satire on poetry, religion etc. A palatable dish, a divine image put together from straw and shavings. Behind it everything becomes farce. Economic nature is true—and *what remains.*

In any case Goethe has treated a recalcitrant subject matter. *Poetic machinery.*
Wilhelm Meister's Apprenticeship, or the pilgrimage to the title of nobility.
Wilhelm Meister is actually a Candide directed against poetry.

29.   My stories and Romantic works are still made too garish and too hard—nothing but rough marks and outlines—naked and undeveloped. They lack that gentle, rounding breath—that fullness of working—middle tints—fine connecting strokes. A certain composure—calm and movement one in the other—individual resolve and distance—suppleness and richness in style—an ear and a hand for appealing chains of sentences.

30.   In a *true speech* one plays all the parts—goes through all characters—through all circumstances—just to achieve a surprise effect—to look at the subject from a fresh angle, to suddenly produce an illusion in the listener, or also to convince him. A speech is an extremely vivid, and intelligent, varying tableau of the inner contemplation of a subject. Now the speaker asks a question, now he answers, then he speaks and engages in dialogue, then he tells a story, then he seems to forget the subject only to suddenly return to it, then he pretends to be convinced, the more cunningly to destroy the case, then disingenuously, emotionally, courageously he turns to his children. He acts as if everything were over and done with—now he speaks to countrymen, now to these or those, even to lifeless objects.
In short, a speech is a drama in monologue.
There are only open, straightforward orators—overblown orators are worth nothing. The true speech is in the style of the high comedy, but interwoven individually with great poetry. Otherwise it is the really clear, simple prose of everyday life—in the style of a dialogue. The orator must be able to assume any tone.

31.   There are people possessed of an obstinate and strange individuality who are not made for matrimony. Married people must have a kind of mixture of independence and its opposite. They must have a firm character, as one would possess *things*, in order to be able to be a *possession*—and yet to be supple, elastic, and thoroughly *determined*, without being obstinate and anxious.

32.   Spinozism is a supersaturation with the divine. Unbelief a lack of the divine sense and of the divine. Thus there are direct and indirect athe-

ists. The more reflective and truly poetic a person is, the more formed and historical his religion will be.

33.   Poetry is *representation* of the *mind*—of the *inner world in its entirety*. Its sole medium, words, indicate this, for they are indeed the outer revelation of that inner realm of energy. They are entirely, what sculpture is to the outer formed world and music is to sounds. Their effect is just the opposite of the inner world—in so far as this is plastic—but there is a musical poetry which sets the mind itself going in a diverse play of movements.

34.   In our mind everything is connected in the most particular, pleasing, and vivid way. The strangest things come together through one place, one time, one strange resemblance, a mistake, some kind of chance. Thus strange unions and peculiar combinations arise—and one thing reminds us of everything—it becomes the sign of many and is itself signified and called forth by many. Understanding and imagination are united in the strangest way by time and space and one can say that each thought, each appearance of our mind is the most individual element of a thoroughly peculiar whole.

35.   The Christian religion is extremely remarkable also in that it so decisively calls on a person's pure goodwill and his actual nature without any schooling, and sets great store by it. It is opposed to learning and art and *actual enjoyment*.
It has its starting point in the common man.
It animates the great majority of what is *limited* on earth.
It is the light that begins to glow in the dark.

36.   The subjects which make up the usual interest of conversation in our cities are at bottom nothing but local events. Prosperity that is more or less the same, the same situation, similar education, the same, moderate character brings about a certain uniformity. Weather, town news, unusual incidents, newspapers, judgments and anecdotes about well-known people, questions of fashion, and at all events news from the seat of the prince, private matters, and some social jokes fill the conversations. Great and general circumstances occupy no one and arouse boredom.
This is certainly better in republics, where the state is the major preoccupation of each person and everyone feels his existence and his needs, his activities and his views to be bound up with the existence and the needs, the activity, and the views of a powerful, extensive society, his life bound

up with a mighty life, and thus he enlarges and exercizes his imagination and his understanding with large subjects and almost involuntarily must forget his narrow self for the sake of the enormous whole.

37.   There has always ever been one illness, and therefore only one universal remedy.[7] With the power of sensation and its organs, the nerves, illness became part of nature. With it freedom, caprice were brought into nature and with it also *sin*, transgression against the will of nature, the cause of all evil. There are purely muscular illnesses which arise from the despotism of the nerves. A moral person must also have a free nature—a recalcitrant kind, one that must be educated, a particular nature. If animal life is a phlogistic process then all illnesses are antiphlogistic processes—disturbances of combustion. Their diversity bears witness to their personal origin. Illness is a conflict of the organs. General illness must almost always become local, just as local illness necessarily becomes general.
Transitoriness, frailty is the character of the kind of nature that is bound up with spirit. It bears witness to the activity and universality, the sublime personality of the spirit.

38.   The more personal, local, temporal, particular a poem is, the nearer it stands to the center of poetry. A poem must be quite *inexhaustible*, like a person and a good saying.
What was the parallelism of oriental poetry?
What was said above of the poem is also true of the novel.
If God could become man he can also become stone, plant, animal, and element, and perhaps in this way there is a kind of continuing salvation in nature.
Individuality in nature is quite infinite. How much this view animates our hopes of the personality of the universe. Remarks on what the ancients called sympathy?
Even our thoughts are effective factors in the universe.
Many people have more a spatial personality—others more a temporal one. Might this be the difference between heroes and artists?
Ought not people to circulate more, like money? Hindus and Chinese originate in a quiet, peaceful domestic life.
Otherwise I will fall into the miserable path of philistinism. Activity will cure me.
It is very probable that in nature too a marvelous number mysticism is taking place. Also in history. Is not everything full of meaning, symmetry, ref-

erence, and strange connection? Cannot God also reveal himself in mathematics, as in every other branch of learning?

The qualities or peculiarities can be determined, for example, through certain times, relations, volumes, outlines, and intensities, and be essentially associated with them.

Ought not logic, the theory of relations, be applied to mathematics?

39.   The idea of philosophy is a mysterious tradition. Philosophy is the very task of *knowing*.

There is an indeterminate science of learning—a mysticism of the very drive to know—like the spirit of learning—therefore not able to be represented—other than in an image or in application—in the complete representation of a special branch of learning.

Now all learning is connected—thus philosophy will never be complete. Only in the complete system of all learning will philosophy be truly visible. From this mystical character of philosophy it can be explained why each person sought in philosophy something different, and why true philosophy could never be represented.

In Schelling's nature philosophy a limited concept of nature and philosophy is presupposed. What might Schelling's nature philosophy actually be?

The system of morality can lay a considerable claim to also being the only possible system of philosophy.

Philosophy can only be represented in practice and cannot, like the activity of genius, be described at all.

Simplification and combination of learning—the transformation of all branches of learning into one is indeed a philosophical task—an absolute demand of the desire to know.

40.   The sense for poetry has much in common with the sense for mysticism. It is the sense for the particular, personal, unknown, mysterious, for that which is to be *revealed*, what necessarily happens by chance. It represents that which cannot be represented. It sees what cannot be seen, feels what cannot be felt etc. Criticism of poetry is a montrosity. It is already difficult to decide whether something is poetry or not, yet there is only a single possible decision. The poet is truly bereft of his senses—instead everything takes place within him. In the truest sense he presents *subject object—mind and world*. From this comes the infinity of a good poem, eternity. The sense for poetry is closely related to the sense of prophecy and the religious, the seer's sense itself. The poet orders, combines,

chooses, invents—and even to himself it is incomprehensible why it is just so and not otherwise.

41.   Illnesses, particularly long-lasting ones, are years of apprenticeship in the art of life and the shaping of the mind. One must seek to use them through daily observations. For is not the life of the educated person a constant challenge to learn? The educated person lives entirely for the future. His life is struggle; his sustenance and purpose learning and art. The more one learns to live no longer in moments but in years etc., the nobler one becomes. The hurried unrest, the petty doings of the spirit are transformed into great, calm, simple, and comprehensive activity, and splendid patience arrives. Religion and morality become ever more triumphant, these founding strongholds of our existence.
Every natural distress is a reminder of a higher home, a higher nature that is more akin to us.

42.   The poet must have the ability to imagine other thoughts, and also to represent thoughts in all kinds of sequences and in the most diverse expressions. As a composer can inwardly imagine different sounds and instruments, can allow them to move before him and combine them in many ways, so that he becomes like the life spirit of these sounds and melodies, as in a similar way a painter, as a master and inventor of colored shapes, knows how to change them at will, place them against and next to one another, to multiply them, and produce all possible kinds and single examples, so too must the poet be capable of imagining the speaking spirit of all things and actions in its different guises, and of perfecting all genres of language arts and animating them with especial, particular meaning. He must invent conversations, letters, speeches, stories, descriptions, passionate utterances filled with all possible subjects, under many different circumstances and spoken by a thousand different people, and commit them to paper in appropriate words. He must be in a position to speak about everything in an entertaining and significant way, and speaking or writing must fill him himself with enthusiasm for speaking and writing.

43.   History is applied morality and religion—also applied *anthropology* in a more general sense. From this comes the marvelous connection of history with our vocation—of Christianity and morality.
We carry the burdens of our fathers as we have received their good, and in this way people indeed live in the whole of the past and the future and nowhere less than in the present.

The Holy Spirit is more than the Bible. He must be our teacher of Christianity—not the dead, earthly, ambivalent letter.

44.   Philosophy is *arbitrary*, like all synthetic science such as mathematics. It is an ideal, self-invented method of observing and ordering etc. the inner world.
Can philosophy even be the unattainable science *kat exochen*—the scientific ideal?

45.   Away with merriment and sadness, funny and touching things—for the sensible person—as well as for the true poet. (Serene, sensible seriousness.)
Songs, epigrams etc. are for poetry what arias, *anglaises* etc. are for music.[8]
Sonatas and symphonies etc.—that is true music.
Poetry too must simply be merely sensible—*artificial*—*invented*—fantastic! etc.
Shakespeare is to me more obscure than Greece. I understand the jokes of Aristophanes—but Shakespeare's not by a long way. Altogether I still understand Shakespeare very imperfectly.
If a joke is to be poetic it must be thoroughly unnatural, a mask.
Even in the theater the principle of imitation of nature still tyrannizes. The value of the play is measured according to it. The ancients understood that much better. With them everything was *more poetic*.
Our theater is thoroughly unpoetic—only operetta and opera approach poetry, and still not in the actors—their acting etc.

46.   In the end the comprehensibility of a phenomenon rests on faith and will.[9] If I make a secret of an appearance, it is that for me. It is with this as it is with limits.

47.   Can miracles bring about conviction? Or would true conviction, this highest function of our mind and our personality, be the only, true, God-proclaiming miracle? Every miracle must stay isolated within us, unconnected with the rest of our consciousness, a dream. But an intense moral conviction, a divine attitude, this would be a real lasting miracle.

48.   Marriage is the highest secret. Marriage with us is a popularized secret. It is bad that with us there is only the choice between marriage and solitude. They are the extremes—but how many people are capable of an actual marriage—how few also can endure solitude. There are unions of

all kinds. Marriage is an infinite union. Is woman the purpose of man and is woman without purpose?

49.   May the realm of the poet be the world, pressed into the focus of his time. May his plan and his execution be poetic, that is, poetic nature. He can use everything, he needs only to amalgamate it with spirit, he must make a whole out of it. He must represent the general as he does the particular—all representation is in the opposite and his freedom to combine makes him unlimited. All poetic nature is nature. All qualities of the latter are fit for it. As individual as it is, it is still of general interest. What use to us are descriptions that leave spirit and heart cold, lifeless descriptions of lifeless nature—they must at least be symbolic, like nature itself, even if they are not to produce any play of the state of the mind. Nature must either be the bearer of ideas, or the mind must be the bearer of nature. This law must be effective in the whole and in detail. The poet may absolutely not appear an egoist. He must himself be appearance. He is the prophet of the imagination of nature, just as the philosopher is the nature prophet of the imagination. To the former, what is objective is everything, to the latter, what is subjective is everything. The former is the voice of the universe, the latter the voice of the most simple unit, the principle; the former is song, the latter speech. The variety of the former unites the infinite, the diversity of the latter combines the most finite. The poet always remains true. He endures in the cycle of nature. The philosopher changes within the eternally enduring. The eternally enduring can only be represented in what is changeable. The eternally changeable only in the lasting, whole, present moment. The images of nature are before and after. It alone is reality. All representation by the poet must be symbolic or moving. Moving here stands for affecting altogether. The symbolic does not affect us immediately, it causes autonomous activity. This stimulates and arouses, the former touches and moves. The former is an action of the spirit, this a suffering of nature, the former goes from appearance to being, this from being to appearance, the former from imagination to intuition, this from intuition to imagination. Formerly the poet could be everything to all men, the circle was still so small, people were still closer in knowledge, experiences, customs, character; such an undemanding person, in this world of simple but stronger demands, raised people so beautifully above themselves, to the feeling of the higher dignity of freedom, excitability was still so new.

Notes

Introduction

1. Cf. Richard Rorty, *Objectivity, Relativism, and Truth* (Cambridge: Cambridge University Press, 1991), p. 22: Pragmatists "do not require either a metaphysics or an epistemology. They view truth as, in William James' phrase, what is good for *us* to believe. So they do not need an account of a relation between beliefs and objects called 'correspondence,' nor an account of human cognitive abilities which ensure that our species is capable of entering into that relation."

2. Cf. Rorty, *Objectivity, Relativism, and Truth*, p. 28: "I think that putting the [reduction of objectivity to solidarity] in such moral and political terms, rather than in epistemological or metaphilosophical terms, makes clearer what is at stake. For now the question is not about how to define words like 'truth' or 'rationality' or 'knowledge' or 'philosophy,' but about what self-image our society should have of itself."

3. Although Noam Chomsky acknowledges the linguistic work of Novalis's contemporary Wilhelm von Humboldt, and marginally also that of his literary associates August Wilhelm and Friedrich Schlegel, as forerunners of modern generative grammar, he makes no mention of Novalis. See *Cartesian Linguistics. A Chapter in the History of Rationalist Thought* (New York and London: Harper and Row, 1966), pp. 16–30.

4. Cf. Steven Pinker, *The Language Instinct* (New York: HarperCollins, 1995), p.18: "Language is a complex, specialized skill, which develops in the child spontaneously, without conscious effort or

formal instruction, is deployed without awareness of its underlying logic, is qualitatively the same in every individual, and is distinct from more general abilities to process information or behave intelligently."

5. Cf. Pinker, *The Language Instinct*, pp. 70–71, 80–82.

6. Nelson Goodman, *Languages of Art: An Approach to the Theory of Symbols* (Indianapolis and New York: Bobbs-Merrill, 1968). See especially Ch. II 8, Modes of Metaphor, and Ch. II 9, Expression.

7. This version of what mental representation can do implies the abandoning of what Richard Rorty calls "the mind as Mirror of Nature." See *Philosophy and the Mirror of Nature* (Oxford: Basil Blackwell, 1980), p. 171: "If we see knowledge as a matter of conversation and of social practice, rather than as an attempt to mirror nature, we will not be likely to envisage a metapractice which will be the critique of all possible forms of social practice."

8. See *Hegel's Phenomenology of Spirit*, trans. A. V. Miller (Oxford: Clarendon Press, 1977), pp. 316–19.

1. Miscellaneous Observations

1. A set of 114 fragments with the title *Pollen* was published in the journal *Athenaeum* at Easter 1798, with the signature "Novalis." This version contained a number of changes and omissions resulting from Friedrich Schlegel's editorial emendations. The text translated is that of the complete manuscript of 125 fragments, headed *Miscellaneous Observations*, which shows Novalis's revisions as well as some additional material. In a letter to Friedrich Schlegel dated December 26, 1797, Novalis describes this collection as "fragments of my continuing dialogue with myself—shoots." His idiosyncratic punctuation, characteristic of all the unpublished notebooks, is generally retained.

2. For an extensive discussion of Novalis's working-out of a theory of signs in his Fichte notebooks of 1795–1796, see Wm. Arctander O'Brien, *Novalis. Signs of Revolution* (Durham and London: Duke University Press, 1995), pp. 77–118. Also more generally Géza von Molnár, *Novalis' "Fichte-Studies." The Foundations of His Aesthetics* (The Hague: Mouton, 1970).

3. This fragment and the next two refer to Erasmus Darwin's *Zoonomia or the Laws of Organic Life* (1794). For Novalis's association of Platonic ideas with Darwin's comment on the dazzling of the eyes on

waking, see my *Athenaeum. A Critical Commentary* (Bern and Frankfurt: Herbert Lang, 1973), p. 24.

4. Goethe's novel *Wilhelm Meister's Apprenticeship* (1795–1796) was hailed as an epoch-making work by the Schlegel circle.

5. The reflections on wit and irony in this section (MO 30, 35, 36) are a response to Friedrich Schlegel's definitions in the latter's "Critical Fragments," published in 1797 in the journal *Lyceum*. See "Critical Fragments" 42, 48, and 56, trans. Peter Firchow, in Friedrich Schlegel, *Philosophical Fragments* (Minneapolis and Oxford: University of Minnesota Press, 1991), pp. 5–7. Wit for Schlegel is a dimension of the Romantic creative ideal of sociability, while irony belongs more centrally in the aesthetic sphere as the quality of self-awareness essential to Romantic writing.

6. The concept of progressivity is fundamental to Romantic literary theory. See *Athenaeum* fragment 116, in Schlegel, *Philosophical Fragments*, pp. 31–32. Cf. MO 42 and 47, also 53, where the idea of the progressive is associated with the enduring eighteenth-century notion of perfectibility.

7. In Friedrich Schlegel's terminology, the "classical" or "objective" was at first contrasted with the "interesting," meaning something like "modern" or what was later to be defined as "Romantic." Cf. Ernst Behler, *German Romantic Literary Theory* (Cambridge: Cambridge University Press, 1993), pp. 103–06. Behler points to Schlegel's association of the "interesting" with the ideal of perfectibility.

8. Influential political theorists of the 1790s such as Kant and Schiller argued that cultivation of the individual should take precedence over the claims of society. See Frederick C. Beiser, *Enlightenment, Revolution, and Romanticism. The Genesis of Modern German Political Thought 1790–1800* (Cambridge, Mass. and London: Harvard University Press, 1992), pp. 17–18. But Novalis's thinking in this regard never loses sight of the moral bond between the individual and the community (cf. MO 81).

9. In the language of alchemy, a universal solvent. As an analogy, used several times in Novalis's notebooks to suggest the flux of ideas and the possibility of new associations.

10. The reference is to the Holy Roman Empire.

11. According to legend, the cries of geese warned the Romans of the attacking Gauls in 390 B.C. Whoever in Germany raises the alarm about the dangers of revolutionary ideas has the right to claim leadership.

12. Novalis implies that the Germans will be the founders of a new, universal, philosophical age, outstripping the more politically active French (see also MO 60).

13. Well-known English merchants of the late eighteenth century.

14. Literary translation was among the major interests of the Romantic circle. August Wilhelm Schlegel was to become celebrated for his translations of Dante and Shakespeare, and Tieck for his version of *Don Quixote*.

15. For Novalis, a truly poetic translation demonstrates the kind of critical reflection needed for Romantic creativity, hence his belief that the translator must be "the poet of the poet." He approved neither of the poet Bürger's attempt at translating Homer into German iambics (1771), nor of Pope's translations into heroic couplets made fifty years earlier.

16. Gr. *misó-theos*, God-hating.

17. Entheism, the oneness of God, a concept employed in theological discussion of the period. See Alexander Gelley's note in his translation of MO as "Miscellaneous Remarks," *New Literary History* 22 (1991), p. 405.

18. Gr. *kat' exochen*, in an absolute sense. For the value of ritual as spectacle, cf. MO 71.

19. Novalis occasionally included distichs such as this one among his philosophical fragments.

20. Archimedes boasted of being able to move the world if he were given a place to stand on. The penetrative power of reflection will allow a comprehensive view of history for the first time.

21. Novalis shared with Friedrich Schlegel the idea of creative chaos, which here is set out as a form of the triadic teleological thinking characteristic of the late eighteenth century in Germany.

22. Novalis's characteristic emphasis on the productive aspect of his fragments contrasts with Friedrich Schlegel's definition of the form as like a small work of art, complete in itself "like a hedgehog."

23. Friedrich Schlegel's essays on Georg Forster and Lessing appeared in 1797 in the journal *Lyceum*. For Novalis's distinction between "plus poetry" or poem, and "minus poetry" or prose, see LFI 45.

24. There are many references in Novalis's notebooks to the ancient doctrine of emanation, whereby all good is understood as flowing

from the divine. Here used figuratively to suggest the participation of every individual in the common spiritual life.

25. Contemporary German professors of philosophy.

26. One learned in the study of man, on the analogy of "geognostic," see MO 121.

27. As in MO 8, Novalis is using terminology derived from the Scottish physician John Brown, whose *Elements of Medicine* (first published in Latin in 1780) was widely read in Germany. According to Brown's theory, living organisms possess an innate quality of "excitability," that is, the capacity to respond to external stimuli. See John Neubauer, *Bifocal Vision. Novalis' Philosophy of Nature and Disease* (Chapel Hill: The University of North Carolina Press, 1971), pp. 24–5: "Brown believed that the health of an organism depended solely on the proper amount of stimulation, sicknesses could therefore arise only from a lack or an overdose of it and had to be one of two types: overstimulation brought the body into a state of excitement called sthenic, while organisms with a debility in stimulation and excitement were said to be asthenic."

28. A widely read literary journal, published in Jena.

29. Macrobiotics, the art or science of prolonging life by bringing its diverse elements into harmony. The title of a medical work by C. W. Hufeland (1797).

30. In his *Reflections on the Revolution in France* (1790), Burke's recognition of justifiable revolutionary change, together with his defence of inherited monarchy and the rule of law, appeared to Novalis to stem from the same kind of radical conservatism as his own.

31. Goethe's verse epic of that name (1797) met with a mixed critical reception.

32. Geognostic, one learned about the earth. The reference is to an ironic comment in *Wilhelm Meister's Apprenticeship* on the ponderousness of the German character (Book IV, ch. 20).

33. These questions, the subject of much contemporary political debate, are further explored in FL.

2. *Logological Fragments I*

1. This selection is from a manuscript dating from the end of 1797 to mid-1798. Some of the material included was crossed out by Novalis

for future revision, other entries (shown by an asterisk) were marked as specially deserving of further work.

2. A central tenet of early Romantic theory. Novalis emphasizes the fruitfulness of this kind of intuitive philosophy, which is facilitated by mutual sympathy.

3. The Romantic circle acknowledged Fichte's introduction of a new philosophical language of great flexibility and imaginativeness, hence "Fichtecizing."

4. Gk. *makrología*, prolixity. This extended comment develops the contrast between the mechanical and the intuitive thinker sketched in LFI 10. It underlines Novalis's conviction, implied in LFI 1, that the history of philosophy is more than a "lexicographical" history of philosophers. Cf. TF 34.

5. The emergence of the synthetic or final term from the two premises of the syllogism is compared to the emergence of a kernel from the parent parts or husk of a seed, illustrating the organic character of philosophy.

6. In speculating on the existence of a higher truth which animates our poetic imagination, Novalis builds on Fichte's distinction between self and nonself in his *Theory of Scientific Knowledge* (1794), but reverses his statement of the way each is determined by the other. Cf. Fichte, *The Science of Knowledge*, ed. and trans. Peter Heath and John Lachs (Cambridge: Cambridge University Press, 1982), pp. 122–27, 218–20.

7. Fragments 25–45 comprise a separate section with the heading "Poetry."

8. The Romantic theory of the novel placed it at the pinnacle of all modern writing. Like the terms of a geometrical progression it is raised to the power of itself and is always open to new development.

9. The comment is in keeping with the Romantic tendency toward fusion of the arts. Cf. LFII 17.

10. This cryptic observation crystallizes the notion that potentiated or transcendental poetry (art poetry) will succeed simple or nature poetry, so that the "symbolic construction of the transcendental world" can begin.

11. In another use of mathematical symbols like the idea of potentiation, Novalis implies that plus-poetry (in the form of the true poem) has the positive, open-ended quality of the unknown or the mysterious, while

minus-poetry (in the form of prose) moves negatively, since its clarity precludes further development. Ultimately, through the action of the *ordo inversus*, plus and minus cancel each other out and prose and poem are one.

12. Fragments 46–50 are grouped under the heading "Poeticisms." For the quality of the interesting, see MO 51.

13. "To Chloe" (1787), text by J. G. Jacobi.

14. This programmatic assertion pinpoints Novalis's intensification of Fichte's distinction between self and nonself, and his vision of the ultimate wholeness of all things. Through the *ordo inversus* the contradiction is dissolved and what seemed fatally distinct becomes one. A little later in the manuscript he writes even more uncompromisingly: "I am You."

15. The most comprehensive definition of Novalis's understanding of the term "Romantic" and of the effects of reflection or potentiation in all aspects of life. The "logarithmic change" is the key to the ultimate resolution of the contradictions between finite and infinite, between present and higher reality.

16. Possibly a play on the word "Romantic," but also implying the vernacular, a language accessible to all.

17. Novalis emphasizes the particularity of his use of the word "soul," implying that the expression "world soul" for him derives from analogy with this. He had not read Schelling's *On the World Soul* (1798) at this time.

18. Cf. LFI 61: In truly pure mathematics "quantities are construed by quantities."

3. Logological Fragments II

1. This section of Novalis's notebooks dates from between May and July 1798. The first 10 entries are headed "Fragments or Mental Tasks." As in LFI, he regarded those marked with an asterisk as worthy of further work.

2. Novalis's interest in the Sanskrit language and Indian mythology stemmed in particular from Georg Forster's translation of the English version of *Sacontalá* (1791, after Sir William Jones).

3. The refraction of light is an image used often by Novalis to evoke the visionary powers derived from experiences such as love, philosophy or, as in the following fragment, magic.

4. Under the heading "Anecdotes," fragments 11–16 take up the subject of narrative. At the same time as he was at work on this manuscript, Novalis began his first prose fiction, *The Apprentices at Saïs*. His notes record his desire to extend the boundaries of both fiction and history writing.

5. Cf. Friedrich Schlegel in *Athenaeum* fragment 146: "Just as the novel colors all of modern poetry, so satire colors and, as it were, sets the tone for all of Roman poetry, yes, even the whole of Roman literature. This poetry surely remained through all its changes a classic universal poetry." *Philosophical Fragments*, pp. 36–37.

6. Georg Christoph Lichtenberg, *Complete Explanation of Hogarth's Engravings* (1794–1799). His commentaries engaged with pyschological and sociological, as well as aesthetic, matters.

7. Cf. LFI 13, where Novalis distinguishes three stages in the history of philosophy. In the first of these one type of thinker is "the crude, intuitive poet."

8. Cf. LFI 65, where the loss of hieroglyphic meaning is deplored. The hieroglyph represented for Novalis a magical language that brings together form, sound and meaning. Cf. Steven Schaber, "Novalis' Theory of the Work of Art as Hieroglyph," in *The Germanic Review* 48 (1973), pp. 35–43.

9. Classification of antithetical kinds of writing is typical of the period. Schiller's essay *On the Naive and Sentimental in Literature* (1795) draws a distinction similar to that between "natural" and "artificial" poetry. Goethe insisted that his *Fairy-Tale* (1795) was to be read not as allegory but as symbol. Cf. LFI 97.

10. A pastime of the eighteenth century where the end rhymes were given and verses had to be written to suit.

11. The motif of the veiled image appears in *The Apprentices at Saïs* at the end of the interpolated fairy tale "Hyacinth and Rose Blossom." When the young pilgrim lifts the veil, he discovers his sweetheart—a poetic statement that the quest for self-knowledge and wisdom finds its goal through love. See Alice A. Kuzniar, "Reassessing Romantic Reflexivity—The Case of Novalis," in *The Germanic Review* 63 (1988), p. 82, for a discussion of this motif.

12. Hebrew, the unpronounced name of God. For Novalis it represents the concept of the name raised to the power of itself, and illustrates the magical function of naming.

13. By the time Novalis was writing, the French Revolutionary armies had established "sister republics" in Belgium, the Rhineland, Holland, and Switzerland, ostensibly at the request of internal sympathizers.

14. The great new idea is presumably his theory of magical idealism.

4. Monologue

1. The date of composition is not known, and the heading "Monologue" was probably added by a later editor.

2. The self-referentiality which is construed in the *Monologue* as the essential characteristic of the highest form of language, that is, poetry, is identified by Novalis also in the purely theoretical nature of mathematics, in the image as a symbol only of itself, and in the task of philosophy to explain itself.

5. Faith and Love or The King and Queen

1. This collection was published in the *Yearbooks of the Prussian Monarchy*, Berlin, in July 1798, again with the signature "Novalis." The first six entries were grouped as a preface. For an analysis of FL in terms of a theory of political obligation, see Beiser, *Enlightenment, Revolution, and Romanticism*, pp. 267–73.

2. An example of Novalis's original intention to disperse poetic couplets among the prose fragments.

3. Said of Henri IV.

4. An instrument for measuring the oxygen content of the air, here figuratively suggesting a healthy, natural moral climate rather than one produced artificially as oxygen can be produced from saltpeter.

5. The symbolism of the mountains and the plain suggests the destructive force of the Revolution in leveling the natural social order.

6. Pyrites or firestone, believed to strike fire. The image is a warning of the dangers of untrammeled democracy, which may bring about a political explosion with unforeseen consequences.

7. The heights represent the place where the monarch has his being; the "lily in the sun" is the queen.

8. The letter or sign is the visible form of a mystical idea. In the same way the constitution or the laws represent the allegiance owed to the mystical sovereign, itself represented in the persons of the royal family.

9. The notion of eternal peace was current as a result of Kant's essay "On eternal peace" (1795). See also FL 42 and LFI 15.

10. The physical and biological imagery used here embodies Novalis's critique of revolutionary action that loses sight of its constructive purpose.

11. *The Battle of the Frogs and Mice*, a mock-heroic Greek poem, is as far removed from the spirit of the *Iliad*, which it parodies, as the external trappings of the (French) republic are from its true spirit. For Novalis the latter means the participation of the whole community in the life of the state.

12. That is, the worth of the queen, who is endowed with special symbolic significance as the mother of the state.

13. A coinage: a measure of morals, on the analogy of "eudiometer."

14. A work in marble by the sculptor Schadow, depicting the queen and her sister, designed for the royal palace in Berlin, but which at this time was not displayed since the king did not admire it.

15. The criticisms of the secular reigns of Frederick II and Frederick William II of Prussia implied in FL 33, 36, and 37 contributed to the controversial character of FL.

16. Novalis employs the classical idea of the golden age to represent the ultimate union of all religion, art, knowledge, and social endeavor in a harmonious whole.

17. In *Wilhelm Meister's Apprenticeship*, Natalie most nearly equates an ideal of womanhood.

18. Fragments 44–68 comprise a separate group headed "Political Aphorisms." They were to appear in the next issue of the journal, but because of the king's known discomfort at what he perceived as the excessively idealistic tone of FL in its depiction of the duties of the monarch, their publication was suppressed by the Prussian censor. Friedrich Schlegel wrote to Novalis that the king was reported to have said: "More is demanded of a king than he is capable of giving. It is always forgotten that he is a human being."

19. This and the following aphorisms employ the Brownian medical terminology of excitability, stimulus, energy, and weakness to illustrate kinds of political debility.

20. Dionysius II, tyrant of Syracuse in the fourth century B.C., and Croesus, last king of Lydia in the sixth century B.C.; both were overthrown and forced into exile.

21. A fluid believed to be a conductor of electricity.

6. Teplitz Fragments

1. Novalis worked on a new manuscript while at the Bohemian spa of Teplitz in the late summer of 1798. On July 29 he wrote to Friedrich Schlegel: "Women, the Christian religion, and everyday life are the central monads of my meditations."

2. The name of a collection of fairy tales by Wieland (1786–1789). Novalis compares the mysterious and beautiful effects of comets with the world of magic.

3. His young fiancée, Sophie von Kühn, died in March 1797. Her name came to represent for Novalis the central life experiences of love and philosophy.

4. To be unable to be raised to the power of itself means for any entity that it lacks progressivity and is incapable of self-knowledge. Women are idealized as inspirational figures removed from the common sphere, impervious to growth and change.

5. Cf. LFI 70, where madness is associated with enthusiasm or spirituality.

6. Novalis expresses irritation with the French-inspired manners of the minor German aristocracy who were the patrons of Teplitz. *Les Femmes* are not to be confused with real women.

7. The Teplitz fragments were stimulated in part by Novalis's reading of the lively but mundane observations of the Prince de Ligne, *Mélanges Militaires, Littéraires, et Sentimentaires* (1795ff.).

8. "Magical idealism" comes to signify Novalis's conception of "making Romantic" (cf. LFI 66) or transcending the fragmentation of the world through poetry and philosophy. In the present context "magical" is contrasted with "empirical," in that what is magical is autonomous and not contingent.

9. The reference could be to the French *Encyclopédie* or any contemporary encyclopedic dictionary.

10. As in the "medical cure" for the French Revolution in TF 2, hypochondria or melancholy is perceived as an interruption of normal health which allows self-appraisal and a fresh beginning.

11. Cf. the king's comment on FL, FL note 18. This fragment echoes the themes of FL.

12. The scientist Erasmus Darwin was among those at the end of the eighteenth century who experimented with keyboard instruments that produced different colors rather than or as well as sounds.

7. On Goethe

1. The essay on Goethe and the notes that follow it were written in the weeks after Novalis's stay in Teplitz. Goethe was revered above all other writers by his German contemporaries, Friedrich Schlegel calling him one of the three great masters of modern literature, with Dante and Shakespeare. But Novalis's discussion is exceptional in its focus on Goethe's scientific writings.

2. By this time Goethe had published *The Metamorphosis of Plants* (1790) as well as a series of essays on optics which are the first results of his studies of color.

3. Novalis compares the insights derived from the historian's perception of the ancient past with those achieved by the scientist in the study of nature. Neither of these kinds of "material" is understood conceptually until the scholar engages with it.

4. Perception of the classical as the other depends on the literary self-consciousness of the modern age. It is analogous to location of the beginning of philosophy in the self-penetration of the spirit.

5. In GD 24 Novalis writes of the need for a critique of all philosophical and scientific criteria.

6. The pathologists of the humors and the nerves respectively. See Neubauer, *Bifocal Vision*, pp. 110–11, on the disputes between the old-fashioned humoral pathologists and the neuropathologists who followed Brown.

7. This part of the manuscript is concerned directly or indirectly with painting and sculpture. In August 1798 Novalis visited the celebrated Dresden Gallery with members of the Schlegel circle, who recorded their own response to this occasion in the *Dialogue on Paintings*, published in the *Athenaeum*. See my *Athenaeum*, pp. 53–76.

8. The reproductions of Greek sculptures in the Gallery prompted Novalis's reflections on the concept of antiquity in the essay on Goethe.

9. This kind of alienation of the categories is essential in making the world Romantic. Friedrich Schlegel conceived of irony in just such contradictory terms, while Novalis speaks of humor as "a free mixture of the conditional and the unconditional" (MO 30).

10. As in OG 23, Novalis evokes possible representations of the potentiation that is the dynamic underlying the Romanticization of the world.

11. These beautiful images express the oneness of all living things, including human beings, and their capacity to dissolve and come together. Cf. GD 46: "All synthesis is a *flame*."

8. General Draft

1. The text translated is a selection from more than one thousand notes made by Novalis between September 1798 and March 1799 toward his project for an encyclopedia. Many entries are classified under a keyword for later sorting. Cf. LFII 31: "The encyclopedic scholar . . . is the maximum of a scholar."

2. As in his metaphorical application of the refraction of light, Novalis here uses unison, dissonance, and harmony as images.

3. The self only becomes conscious of its beginning from the perspective of maturity, and then constructs itself like a work of art. The argument parallels that concerning our conceptualization of antiquity and nature in OG. See also GD 3.

4. In his creative writing as well as in his notebooks, Novalis sought to bring together the genres of novel and fairy tale in a single Romantic form.

5. This lamentable observation can be explained, if not excused, by the reification of women revealed in TF.

6. The note reflects Novalis's reading on astrology and Eastern mysticism. The interconnection between sign and signified provides an instance of his theory of mutual representation.

7. The fairy tale can represent a magical world, free of causation, unlike the traditional novel which depicts the everyday.

8. Cf. GD 2 and MO 94 on progressive chaos.

9. The principle of magical idealism requires the distinction between self and nonself, external and internal experience, to fall away.

10. That is, self and nonself.

11. The gradation of musical pitch now becomes a metaphor for our perception of the world and ourselves.

12. Cf. Novalis's citing of Hemsterhuis and the concept of moral astronomy in his Teplitz letter to Schlegel. See Introduction.

13. Cf. MO 73 on the mediator in religion.

14. A poetic statement of the way to overcome the barrier between self and nonself. Cf. GD 16, on the potential to become God.

15. Gk. *makro-anthropos*, man writ large, on the analogy of "macrocosm."

16. "Polar" here has the sense of "antithetical." The "polar sphere" is that phase of consciousness where the antinomies are recognized simultaneously, so preparing the way for their resolution in the golden age.

17. The magical idealist does not arrive at truth by a process of logic or cognition. He refracts (spiritual) light as a prism does, by virtue of his simple existence.

18. The reference is to Kant's disparaging remarks about the "mysticism" of the pietists and Moravian Brethren in his *Conflict of the Faculties* (1798). Novalis compares dynamic religious feeling to physical processes.

19. In FL Novalis constructs an image of the ideal monarchy. Other desired ends such as eternal peace, the golden age, magic, and morality are endowed with potential being in their representations. "Here or nowhere is America" is an expression from *Wilhelm Meister's Apprenticeship*, Bk. 7, ch. 3, where "America" stands for the ideal society of the future.

9. *Christendom or Europe*

1. In September 1799 Novalis received a copy of Schleiermacher's *Speeches on Religion*. The theologian stressed contemplation and feeling in religious experience, and the importance of historical insight to bring about spiritual renewal. The rhetorical character of CE makes it unique in Novalis's writing. The work is conceived as a kind of sermon on a new religion for modern Europe, when the barriers of schism, nationalism, revolution, and war are overcome. The essay remained unpublished.

2. Novalis introduces his theme of the political and religious unity of Europe in pointing to its symbol in the Pope of medieval Christendom. The guild of the priesthood acted as an intermediary between the people and the supreme authority.

3. The fatherland signifies that inner or better world which is the home of the spirit and which is to be sought in art and nature.

4. The admiration of the Romantic circle for Raphael's Sistine Madonna, the centerpiece of the Dresden Gallery, is echoed here. In the third of the *Hymns to the Night*, a vision of his transfigured dead bride appears, Madonna-like, to the poet.

5. Devotion to relics of the saints and pilgrimage to their shrines can be compared to the adoption of visible symbols of the state, which is advocated in FL 19 and 26.

6. The sending of Christian missionaries to the New World illustrates a universalizing process that Novalis saw as the path to making the world Romantic.

7. In the context of Novalis's (and Schleiermacher's) privileging of intuitive feeling, Copernicus and Galileo represent the destructive use of reason that undermines response to the transcendental and sets up resistance to the religious and creative impulse. They are empiricists rather than magical idealists (cf. TF 33).

8. The commercial spirit, praised in MO 67 and GD 51, goes hand in hand with the aspirations of the proselytizing Church, and is a dimension of that progressivity that Novalis praised as the dynamic of history.

9. In the mythic construction of Novalis's historical narrative, this moment represents the loss of innocence and the end of the original golden age.

10. The Reformation, in this context the outward sign of the disintegration of the ideal of medieval Christendom.

11. "Faith and love" here represents the early idealism which has been lost, while the seasonal imagery suggests that, like the golden age, it can return.

12. This playful mention of "the gods" may have been prompted by the heroic landscapes Novalis saw in the Dresden Gallery. The term was commonly used both in the classical sense and unspecifically. Cf. OG 26.

13. These ideas on historical change, confirmed in Novalis's thinking by his reading of Schleiermacher, lead into his analysis of the French Revolution and show why he applauded Burke's radical conservatism.

14. Martin Luther.

15. Novalis was reading Luther's works at this time, as a number of entries in the notebooks for 1799–1800 record. There too he makes a distinction between Lutheranism and Protestantism.

16. Count Zinzendorf was the founder of the religious community of the Moravian Brethren, to which Novalis's father adhered. The seventeenth-century Silesian mystic Jacob Böhme was especially revered by the Romantic circle, and Novalis turned to an intensive study of his work soon after writing CE.

17. The Society of Jesus, founded by St. Ignatius Loyola in 1534 to spearhead the Counter-Reformation, is evoked here as a model of universalism.

18. A reference to secret societies such as the Rosicrucians, thought to be modeled on the Jesuit order.

19. The Jesuits were expelled from most European countries between 1773, when the order was dissolved by Pope Clement XIV, and 1814, when it was reinstated.

20. Novalis depicts the Enlightenment as inimical to religious faith in its eclecticism and tolerance, as well as its valorization of secular knowledge.

21. The image of the "monstrous mill" refers to the philosophy of deism, which did not admit revealed religion or the continuing presence of God in creation.

22. The play of colors in refraction is an image of potentiated discovery, but those interested only in its mathematical aspects are blind to this dimension.

23. As a progressive dynamic, history cannot be captured in banal descriptions of "domestic and family life" (as in many novels of the 1790s). History must be understood as a living tradition.

24. Here the destructive power of wit is emphasized. Cf. MO 30: "Wit points to disturbed equilibrium."

25. The second Reformation is the movement that will overturn "modern unbelief." Its first sign is the French Revolution: the observation introduces the essay's positive assessment of this moment of "anarchy" for the future of Europe.

26. Spiritual and social regeneration will only occur if it is inspired by consciousness of the higher realm, that is, by religion free of sectarianism.

27. The reference is to Robespierre's defence of the right to worship and his Cult of the Supreme Being, which was briefly promulgated in 1794.

28. The theophilanthropists were a fashionable sect of French deists during the late 1790s.

29. A reference to Napoleon's Egyptian campaigns of 1798–1799.

30. Cf. MO 63 and 66, where a German cultural renaissance is foreshadowed, which will also have universal meaning.

31. According to legend, Heracles in his cradle strangled two serpents which the jealous Hera had sent to kill him.

32. A messiah born within the hearts of the faithful becomes a metaphor for the coming of the new golden age.

33. While "mechanics" in Novalis's notebooks can refer to physical phenomena such as centrifugal and centripetal force, here it is an image of the integration of all art, science, religion, and history.

34. The reference is probably to the persistence of the classical tradition since the Renaissance and its uneasy relationship with Christianity.

35. The almost ecstatic tone of this passage is designed to move readers (or listeners) to aspire to their own initiation into the new religion. The imagery is reminiscent of *The Apprentices at Saïs* where the pilgrim seeks sacred knowledge hidden behind a veil.

36. The comment has multiple reference in that, as well as being an image of the Virgin Mary, it suggests the way the draperies of classical sculpture enhance the human figure. Novalis's interest in this subject was stimulated by the antiquities in the Dresden Gallery, as well as by Herder's essay *On Sculpture* (1778). The "brother" who made a new veil for the Virgin is Schleiermacher (*Schleier*, veil), to whose *Speeches on Religion* Novalis now acknowledges a debt as the model for his own essay.

37. A reference to Goethe, described in OG as "the first physicist of his age."

38. Novalis posits a political work comparable in authority and influence to Fichte's *Theory of Scientific Knowledge*.

39. Pope Pius VI died in August 1799 in exile in France, where he had been imprisoned since the defeat of Rome by the French armies early in 1798.

10. Last Fragments

1. These are a selection from notebook entries which Novalis made between May 1799 and November 1800.

2. The mathematical analogy points to Novalis's belief that, together, life and death make up the wholeness of existence. It also is a summation of his theory of mutual representation. Cf. MO 15.

3. CE, which he referred to as a speech, illustrates Novalis's interest in the way oratory is designed to produce a response in the listener. See also LaF 30.

4. In his "sermon" CE, Novalis adopts an evocative, imprecise style of narrative comparable to that in folk tales or legends.

5. Novalis devised experiments in the recently discovered techniques of animal magnetism and galvanism with members of his family.

6. These and later criticisms show how much Novalis has now distanced himself from the Schlegel circle's praise of the work. His *Heinrich von Ofterdingen* was conceived as truly Romantic art, in part to counter Goethe's novel.

7. In his journal for July 27, 1800, Novalis notes his worsening health and his troubled state of mind.

8. *Anglaise*, a dance form popular in instrumental suites, perceived by Novalis as frivolous.

9. Fragments 46–49 are of uncertain date.

Select Bibliography

Behler, Ernst. *German Romantic Literary Theory*. Cambridge: Cambridge University Press, 1993.

Beiser, Frederick C. *Enlightenment, Revolution, and Romanticism. The Genesis of Modern German Political Thought*. Cambridge, Mass. and London: Harvard University Press, 1992. Chapter 11: "The political theory of Novalis," 264–78.

———. *The Fate of Reason. German Philosophy from Kant to Fichte*. Cambridge, Mass. and London: Harvard University Press, 1987.

Brown, Marshall. *The Shape of German Romanticism*. Ithaca: Cornell University Press, 1979.

Chomsky, Noam. *Cartesian Linguistics. A Chapter in the History of Rationalist Thought*. New York and London: Harper and Row, 1966.

Fichte, Johann Gottlieb. *Early Philosophical Writings*. Trans. Daniel Breazeale. Ithaca: Cornell University Press, 1988.

———. *The Science of Knowledge*. Ed. and trans. Peter Heath and John Lachs. Cambridge and New York: Cambridge University Press, 1982.

Friedrichsmeyer, Sara. *The Androgyne in Early German Romanticism: Friedrich Schlegel, Novalis, and the Metaphysics of Love*. Bern: Lang, 1983.

Goodman, Nelson. *Languages of Art: An Approach to the Theory of Symbols*. Indianapolis and New York: Bobbs-Merrill, 1968.

Haywood, Bruce. *Novalis: The Veil of Imagery. A Study of the Poetic Works of Friedrich von Hardenberg.* 's-Gravenhage: Mouton, 1959.

Hegel's Phenomenology of Spirit. Trans. A. V. Miller. Oxford: Clarendon Press, 1977.

Kant, Immanuel. *Conflict of the Faculties.* Trans. and introduction by Mary J. Gregor. New York, NY: Abaris Books, 1979.

———. *Philosophical Writings.* Ed. Ernst Behler with a foreword by René Wellek. New York: Continuum, 1986.

Kuzniar, Alice. *Delayed Endings. Nonclosure in Novalis and Hölderlin.* Athens, Ga. and London: University of Georgia Press, 1987.

———. "Reassessing Romantic Reflexivity—The Case of Novalis." *The Germanic Review* 63 (1988): 77–86.

Lacoue-Labarthe, Philippe and Jean-Luc Nancy. *The Literary Absolute: The Theory of Literature in German Romanticism.* Trans. with an introduction and additional notes by Philip Barnard and Cheryl Lester. Albany: State University of New York Press, 1988.

Mahoney, Dennis F. *The Critical Fortunes of a Romantic Novel. Novalis's "Heinrich von Ofterdingen."* Columbia, SC: Camden House, 1994.

Molnár, Géza von. *Novalis' "Fichte Studies." The Foundation of His Aesthetics.* The Hague: Mouton, 1970.

———. *Romantic Vision, Ethical Context. Novalis and Artistic Autonomy.* Minneapolis: University of Minnesota Press, 1987.

Neubauer, John. *Bifocal Vision. Novalis' Philosophy of Nature and Disease.* Chapel Hill: The University of North Carolina Press, 1971.

———. *Novalis.* Boston: Twayne, 1980.

Novalis. "Aphorisms and Fragments." Trans. Alexander Gelley. In *German Romantic Criticism.* Ed. A Leslie Willson, 62–83. New York: Continuum, 1982.

———. "From Miscellaneous Writings." "Monologue." "Dialogues." "On Goethe." "Studies in the Visual Arts." Trans. Joyce Crick. In *German Aesthetic and Literary Criticism: The Romantic Ironists and Goethe.* Ed. Kathleen M. Wheeler. Cambridge: Cambridge University Press, 1984.

———. "Miscellaneous Remarks." Trans. Alexander Gelley. *New Literary History* 22 (1991): 383–406.

O'Brien, Wm. Arctander. *Novalis. Signs of Revolution.* Durham and London: Duke University Press, 1995.

Pfefferkorn, Kristin. *Novalis. A Romantic's Theory of Language*. New Haven: Yale University Press, 1988.

Pinker, Steven. *The Language Instinct*. New York: HarperCollins, 1995.

Rorty, Richard. *Objectivity, Relativism, and Truth*. Cambridge: Cambridge University Press, 1991.

———. *Philosophy and the Mirror of Nature*. Oxford: Basil Blackwell, 1980.

Schaber, Steven. "Novalis' Theory of the Work of Art as Hieroglyph." *The Germanic Review* 48 (1973): 35–43.

Schlegel, Friedrich. *Philosophical Fragments*. Trans. Peter Firchow. Minneapolis and Oxford: University of Minnesota Press, 1991.

Seyhan, Azade. *Representation and Its Discontents. The Critical Legacy of German Romanticism*. Berkeley and Los Angeles: University of California Press, 1992.

Stoljar, Margaret. *Athenaeum. A Critical Commentary*. Bern and Frankfurt am Main: Herbert Lang, 1973.

Index

This index excludes references to secondary literature on Novalis.

55, 65; as highest form of language, 10; history of, 57; as key to philosophy, 54, 79, 117; lyric, 57, 58, 65; minus, 42, 57; and mysticism, 162; natural, 10–11, 57, 71; purpose of, 56; transcendental, 56–57; union with prose, 57

Pollen. See Miscellaneous Observations
prejudice, 30
prince, 86; as artist, 95–96; as genius of the age, 36–37
progressivity, 7, 30, 131, 140, 169n. 6
proofs of God, 135
Protestantism, 18, 140–142
Prussia, 91, 95; government of, 93

queen: as center of the court, 91–92; duties of, 90; idealization of, 16–17; as model, 92; as mother of the state, 176n. 12

reader: as extension of author, 45–46; writer as, 108
reflection, 26, 30; Romantic theory of, 6; in philosophy, 50
Reformation, 18, 139–141, 181n. 10
religion, 38, 55, 102, 104, 122, 128, 155; ancient, 57; born of anarchy, 18, 145–146; Catholic, 109, 137–139, 141, 151; Christian, 101, 104, 160; in France, 146–147; future, 147–148, 151–152; Greek, 34; and history, 163; Judaism, 35; mediator in, 13, 35; pietist, 2, 134, 180n. 18; prayer, 36; sun-worship, 102
representation, 7, 10, 26, 121, 134, 179n. 10; autonomy of, 12; mutual, 12, 125, 165, 179n. 6, 184n. 2; in series, 116, 117; as tragedy and comedy, 57
republic, 17, 94, 160, 176n. 11; and monarchy, 89, 125; representations of, 90; universal, 36; and youth, 98
revolution, 86, 87, 96, 146, 176n. 10. *See also* French Revolution
Romantic fragment, 2, 4, 44, 81, 168n. 1, 170n. 22; as literary seedings, 3–4, 5, 42

Romantic circle, 2, 3–4, 6–7, 11, 15, 17, 170n. 14, 172n. 3, 181n. 4. *See also* Schlegel, Friedrich
Romanticization, 6, 13–14, 16, 124, 153, 173n. 15; in fairy tale, 125–126; of the world, 19, 60, 177n. 8, 179n. 9, 181n. 6
Rorty, Richard, 5, 12; *Objectivity, Relativism, and Truth,* 167nn. 1, 2; *Philosophy and the Mirror of Nature,* 168n. 7

Schelling, Friedrich Wilhelm Joseph, 3, 162; *On the World Soul,* 173n. 17
Schiller, Friedrich von, 2, 169n. 8; *On the Naive and Sentimental in Literature,* 174n. 9
Schlegel, Friedrich, 2, 6, 13, 19, 42, 117–118, 168n. 1, 169nn. 5, 6, 7, 170nn. 21, 22, 23, 174n. 5, 177n. 1; on irony, 29; theory of the novel, 11, 69; review of *Wilhelm Meister's Apprenticeship,* 15
Schleiermacher, Friedrich, 148–149; *Speeches on Religion,* 18, 180n. 1, 181n. 7, 183n. 36
science: as art, 77; magical, 19, 122, 125; new, 149; and philosophy, 14, 77; questioning of, 16
self, 6, 20; consciousness of itself, 5–6, 10, 107; construction of, 123, 179n. 3; discovery of, 26, 52, 76; higher, 53; limitation of, 133; and nonself, 7, 12, 53, 59, 121, 127, 135, 172n. 6, 173n. 14, 180n. 10; principle of, 135; transcending itself, 6, 28, 64
self-education, 31–32, 53, 74
self-knowledge, 4, 6, 8, 61
senses, 26, 34, 61, 128; mastery over, 76; and sleep, 128; tools of, 39
sexuality, 124–125, 128, 154, 157
Shakespeare, William, 164; *Hamlet,* 66
slavery, 97
social responsibility, 5
society, 32, 36, 106; as communal living, 30; and individual, 169n. 8; and institutions, 30; pure spirit of, 99